MW00716318

Legends Told in Canada

Edith Fowke

RŎM
Royal Ontario Museum

First published in 1994 by the Royal Ontario Museum
100 Queen's Park, Toronto, Ontario M5S 2C6

Canadian Cataloguing in Publication Data
Main entry under title:
Legends told in Canada

Includes bibliographical references.
ISBN 0-88854-410-3

I. Legends - Canada. I. Fowke, Edith, 1913-
II. Royal Ontario Museum.

GR113.L44 1994   398.2'0971   C93-095306-1

Care has been taken to trace the ownership of any copyright material contained in this text. The publishers welcome any information that will enable them to rectify, in subsequent editions, any incorrect or omitted reference or credit.

Title page image: *Church Ornament,* moulded sawdust, J. B. Baret, Quebec, 1843. Sigmund Samuel Trust.

Printed and bound in Canada

Contents

Acknowledgements

I would like to thank Dwight Whalen, Philip Hiscock, and Gary Butler who helped in various ways, and to the collectors and historians from whose writings the stories come.

I must acknowledge a special debt to John Robert Colombo whose books, especially *Mysterious Canada,* were invaluable in suggesting legends and sources, and who also supplied information.

I am grateful for the support of the Publications Department of the Royal Ontario Museum, particularly Sandra Shaul, Head; Glen Ellis, Managing Editor; Barbara Brose, Picture Editor; and Vickie Vasquez-O'Hara, Designer.

Thanks also to my husband, who did not complain during the many months I was working on this book.

Permission has been granted to use the following copyright passages: "Thompson Has a Dirk," from C. I. N. MacLeod, *Stories from Nova Scotia* (Antigonish: Formac, 1974). By permission of Iona MacLeod; "A Duel in Annapolis Royal," from Helen Creighton, *Bluenose Ghosts* (Toronto: Ryerson Press, 1957). This story has been retitled. By permission of the Canadian Museum of Civilization; "The Witch Doctor of Long Point," from Harry B. Barrett, *Lore and Legends of Long Point* (Toronto: Burns and MacEachern, 1977). By permission of Harry B. Barrett; "The Witch of Plum Hollow," from Ruth McKenzie, *Leeds and Grenville: Their First Two Hundred Years* (Toronto: McClelland and Stewart, 1967). By permission of Ruth Mackenzie; "The Mackenzie River Ghost," from Roderick MacFarlane, "Ghost Story," *The Beaver,* Dec. 1986-Jan. 1987. By permission of Christopher Dafoe; "A Pot of Gold," from Laurel Doucette, ed. *Cultural Retention and Demographic Change: Studies of the Hebridean Scots in the Eastern Townships of Quebec.* Canadian Centre for Folk Culture Studies. National Museum of Man, Mercury Series, No. 34. (Ottawa: National Museums of Canada, 1980). By permission of the Canadian Museum of Civilization;

4

"Crippen's Curse," from Wayland Drew, *A Sea Within: The Gulf of St. Lawrence.* (Toronto: McClelland and Stewart, 1984). By permission of Wayland Drew; "The Story of the *Newfoundland,*" from MacEdward Leach, *Songs from the Outports of Newfoundland.* (New York: Folkways, 1966). By permission of MacEdward Leach; "The Ghosts of Mackenzie House," from the *Toronto Telegram,* 28 June 1960. By permission of Andrew MacFarlane.

Introduction

Legends are hard to define. The most extensive study was *American Folk Legend: A Symposium,* based on a 1971 symposium organized by Wayland Hand, the greatest American authority on legends and superstitions. In the opening paper Robert Georges described the generally accepted definition: a story or narrative, set in the recent or historical past, that is believed to be true by those who tell it or by those to whom it is told. He then went on to point out that a legend is not always a story, it is not always set in the recent or historical past, and it is not always believed. As Hand put it, "Folk legends seem endless in bulk and variety, and they are often so short and formless as to defy classification." Despite this confusion, it is usually not difficult to recognize legends.

Sometimes legends are confused with myths. Georges noted: "What is a legend in one time and place may be a myth in another time and place and a märchen in yet another time and place." Nevertheless, general distinctions can be made. Both legends and myths are believed by the people who tell them, or at least are or were originally believed by some people. But where myths deal with supernatural beings, other worlds, and prehistoric times, legends are usually set in this world in historic times, and they normally feature human beings, although they may also involve supernatural creatures such as the devil, ghosts, or fairies.

Ordinary folktales or märchen, while they have much in common with legends, are clearly fictional, and are not believed. Legends, on the other hand, may have some basis in fact. Folklorist Linda Dégh commented: "The two genres, sharing a common stock of narrative motifs, differ in the use of these motifs as their building blocks. The märchen incorporates them into an artistic story, the legend uses them as credible facts." Jacob Grimm made this distinction: "The märchen is more poetic, the legend more historic."

Legends commonly contain traditional motifs, and while no criteria fit all legends, there are various characteristics that help to identify them. As Georges put it, "The legend *may* involve divine or semidivine beings; it *may* be concerned with supernatural or preternatural phenomena; it may be sacred or semi-sacred; it may be told in the first person as an actual account of a personal experience; it *may* provide some explanation for, or account for, the origins of some perceivable phenomenon, action or state." He emphasizes that these characteristics are optional, not obligatory, but they do help to identify legends, and the stories in this book illustrate several of them.

In the course of his work on an index of American legends, Wayland Hand usefully classified legends into (fairly broad) subject categories. His first grouping is creatures of lower mythology, wolves and vampires, fairy folk, and witchcraft and devil lore. Canadians have told many stories of the devil and quite a few about witches, both good and bad. Some parts of the country have many fairy legends, and most regions have some tales of strange creatures. This book has a number of tales of witches: "La Corriveau," "The Witch Doctor of Long Point," and "The Witch of Plum Hollow."

His second group is ghostlore and the realm of the dead. Canada has no shortage of ghost stories and reports of poltergeist hauntings. "The Ghosts of Mackenzie House" is one illustration.

Legends involving Christian religious lore—saints' legends, divine providence, sinners and mockers—comprise the third category. This type is less common in Canada, although Quebec has preserved many saints' legends, and a few from other regions involve religious motifs. "The Death of Father de la Brosse" is a religious legend.

Hand recognized native folklore and mythology as a separate study, largely distinct from the Euro-American tradition. There are, of course, certain points of overlapping. In this collection Tlingit creation myth and Euro-native contact merge in "The Tlingit Encounter with La Pérouse."

Dr. Hand's next listing is treasure legends, and he noted: "Legends dealing with lost mines amount to a major legendary tradition." Canada has a great many of these, mostly involving Captain Kidd's supposed treasure and lost mines, the main ones being "The Lost Lemon Mine," and the McLeod mine of "Headless Valley." An example in this book is "The Pot of Gold."

Hand's groupings of etiological and miscellaneous legends are less relevant to the stories chosen here, but Canada does have a few that are explanatory, and some that could be classified as miscellaneous. He does not mention the modern tales variously known as urban or belief legends, but they have become the most common legends circulating today.

Hand's final category is historical legends. The historical legends presented in this book are some of the most distinctively Canadian of our folktales. Although many folktales told in Canada came from other lands or have parallels internationally, legends are more apt to be linked to a particular place or situation, and therefore reflect a country's history and culture more than other folktales. We do have a number of international legends, although they are often adapted to a Canadian setting. But there are a great many legends related to particular people, places, and events that are distinctively Canadian. These are the ones that are emphasized here.

By "historical legends" I do not mean important events covered in history books, but stories that originate in a definite time and place, and that usually involve real people. Historical persons who inspired legends given here include Sir Humphrey Gilbert, Jean-Pierre Lavallée, Father Jean-Baptiste de la Brosse, Marie-Josephte Corriveau, Sir John Franklin, Tecumseh, John Montgomery, William Lyon Mackenzie, and Dr. Hawley Crippen the wife-killer. Other real but less well known persons who appear here are La Pérouse, Dr. Troyer, and Mother Barnes. Some of the tales reflect specific historical events such as the settlement of Newfoundland, the War of 1812, and the American Civil War.

Some of the stories have not had general circulation and have therefore not acquired the variations that most legends do; these may be family stories or personal-experience narratives, *memorats* rather than full-fledged legends. However, in his list of possible variations Dr. Hand noted that a legend "may be told as a first-person account of a personal experience," and some of these are included if they involve traditional motifs.

Historian Richard Dorson defined historical legends in terms of their source. Those reported orally he called folk legends, those found in print, literary legends, and those that travel back and forth between print and oral transmission, popular legends. This book contains examples of all three kinds.

Transcriptions of oral accounts are usually available only for more recent legends. I prefer these first-hand versions and have used them whenever possible. In such instances the story is given in the words of the people who told it, using the form "Told by — —." Where such an account is unavailable, the one from print that seems closest to a folk version is used, headed as "Reported by — —" or, sometimes, "Based on ——." The stories are arranged in approximate chronological order.

Several of the original texts cited were burdened by eccentricities of punctuation, paragraphing, and capitalization. As a courtesy to the general reader, minor alterations have been made where clarity was impeded. A detailed bibliography is included for those who wish to inspect the original texts "blot for blot."

Background notes introducing the stories are italicized, as are the occasional postscripts included. The narrator or reporter and, when available, the date of the report are included with each story.

Flying Dragon Weathervane, sheet iron, anonymous, Quebec, mid 19th century. Sigmund Samuel Trust.

An Early Account of a Canadian Sea Serpent (1583)

European explorers were the first to write of Canada, and the earliest non-native folk legend was probably this report of a sea serpent sighted off Canada's eastern coast by Elizabethan navigator Sir Humphrey Gilbert (1539?-1583). Similar creatures appear in many legends from many different bodies of water, from Scotland's Loch Ness monster to Canada's Ogopogo.

   This story first appeared in Richard Hakluyt's The Principall Navigations, Voiages, and Discoveries of the English Nation (1589). Hakluyt's three-volume, expanded version of this work (1598-1600) was described by historian J. A. Froude as "the prose epic of the English nation," and by the poet John Masefield as "a great and noble poem."

   Gilbert and the men in four other ships with him all claimed to have seen the monster when they were on the Grand Banks, near Cape Race. They had just turned away from Newfoundland to return to England. I don't know how his log survived, but it is a fact that, nine days later, Gilbert's ship ran into a storm and sank. Legend has it that the serpent resented Gilbert's appearance and wrecked his vessel.

Told by Sir Humphrey Gilbert, 1583

So upon Saturday in the afternoone the 31 of August, we changed our course, and returned backe for England, at which very instant, even in winding about, there passed along betweene us and towards the land which we now forsooke a very lion to our seeming, in shape, hair and colour, not swimming after the maner of a beast by mooving of his feete, but rather sliding upon the water with his whole body (excepting the legs) in sight, neither yet diving under and againe rising above the water, as the maner is, of Whales, Dolphins, Tunise, Porpoises, and all other fish: but confidently showing himselfe above water without hiding.

Notwithstanding, we presented our selves in open view and gesture to amaze him, as all creatures will be commonly at a sudden gaze and sight of men. Thus he passed along turning his head to and fro, yawning and gaping wide, with ougly demonstration of long teeth, and glaring eies, and to bidde us a farewell (coming right against the *Hinde*) he sent forth a horrible voyce roaring or bellowing as doeth a lion, which spectacle we all beheld so farre as we were able to discerne the same, as men prone to wonder at every strange thing, as this doubtlesse was, to see a lion in the Ocean sea, or fish in shape of a lion. What opinion others had thereof, and chiefly the Generall himself, I forbeare to deliver: but he tooke it for Bonum Omen, rejoicing that he was to warre against such enemie, if it were the devil.

Princess Sheila (1600s)

According to a widespread Newfoundland legend, one of the earliest settlers in the Carbonear area was an Irish woman known as Sheila Na Geira or Mageela. She was said to be a princess, or at least of noble blood, and her husband was an Englishman named Gilbert Pike. The many Pike families in Newfoundland claim descent from them.

The legend has turned up in many forms, oral and written. Some versions say that Gilbert Pike was a pirate; the story preserved in the Pike family does not mention the piracy. P. J. Wakeham, a Newfoundland writer, incorporated the legend in a novel.

There is some historical evidence for the story. The Pike family is listed among the earliest settlers around Carbonear, and the pirate in this story, Peter Easton, originally an English sea captain who became a pirate, is known to have visited Newfoundland early in the seventeenth century. A gravestone in Carbonear bears the inscription "Sheila Na Geira Pike, wife of Gilbert Pike, and daughter of John Na Geira, King of County Down, Ireland, died on August 14th, 1753, at the age of one hundred and five years."

Philip Hiscock, archivist of Memorial University's Folklore and Language Archive in St. John's, has studied the various versions of this legend to show how its details have served to bolster Newfoundlanders' pride in their island. He suggested this version by a Carbonear businessman and historian as one of the most complete.

From tradition handed down by the Pike family, from whom there can be nothing more reliable, the mother of the first white child was called Sheila Nagira, a young Irish lady belonging to the aristocracy—who was being sent by her friends in Ireland to France to go into a convent to finish her education under care of her aunt, who was an abbess.

On her voyage this ship was captured by a Dutch warship. This Dutchman was in turn captured by three British warships, sailing under letters of marque with 1175 soldiers, besides their crews, commanded by no other than the redoubtable Peter Easton, who was then on a voyage to Newfoundland, and he landed his captives at Harbour Grace. Peter Easton was at that time sailing in the British service. His success with profit and spoils led him with so many others at that time into piracy and disobedience to the British admiralty.

The lieutenant or second-in-command of this squadron was Albert Pike, who belonged to one of the best West of England families. He fell in love with this young lady, which was reciprocated, and they were married by the chaplain of the fleet. They decided to remain in Newfoundland rather than continue the voyage. They took up their residence in Mosquito, where the best houses were built, and there was born the first white child in Newfoundland. This was prior to Guy's arrival and settlement.

The traditions always say that Sheila Nagira was looked upon as an Irish princess from Connaught, and every Irishman frequenting Newfoundland would make obeisance to her whenever they saw her. The Pike claim descent from her.

Sampler, linen tabby with silk petit point, anonymous, England, 1600-1650. Anonymous gift.

The Soldier~Peasant's Vision (1690)

Edward Farrer's article titled "The Folk Lore of Lower Canada" in the Atlantic Monthly *in April 1882 presented some of the earliest English-language reports of French-Canadian legends. This one, about the appearance of Saint Anne to a French soldier, is typical of the many Quebec legends involving saints.*

Reported by Edward Farrer, 1882

Of the legends growing out of the religious fervour of the habitant, this is now the place to speak. One apparition of St. Anne is preserved in an old rhyme. The Carignan regiment, which was disbanded at Quebec, had served with other French troops on the side of the Emperor Leopold against the Turks, and had borne a conspicuous part in the decisive victory achieved over them by Montecucculi at St. Gothard in Hungary. This legend is entitled "The Soldier-Peasant's Vision," and related the appearance of St. Anne to one of the Carignan soldiers, many of whom took up land in the Isle of Orleans and other islands below Quebec. The original, of which the following is a close translation, was written, it will be observed, before the English conquest of Quebec.

All by the broad St. Lawrence, a hundred years ago,
The Angelus was ringing from the bells of Île-au-Roux;
The reaper leaned upon his scythe, the wild-bee ceased its hum,
The consecrated river hushed its water and was dumb;
The oxen as at Bethlehem knelt of their own accord,
While the incense of the mid-day prayer was wafted to their Lord!
"O good Saint Anne, I swear to thee, thou guardian of my race,"
Cried the bareheaded reaper, while tears bedewed his face,
"For sovereign, for seigneur, for those in high command,
France, with her vines and olives, is in sooth a pleasant land;
But fairer than lily on her shield is the New World colony
Where the weary serf may stand erect, unawed by tyranny!

"Do thou ask the Blessed Virgin to bless our sire, the King,
To overthrow his enemies, bless him in everything;
To speed his royal banners, crown them with victory,
As when we fought the Paynim on the plains of Hungary!
But, O mother of all Bretons, by thy love for Mary's son,
By His agony and dolours, by His wounds on Calvary won,
Guard thou New France from tyrants, oh spare her virgin soil
From the hell of the oppressor, from tumult and turmoil!"

Saint Anne had heard the veteran's prayer, and stood upon the tide,
An aureole about her brow, and angels by her side.
"Fear not, my son," she sweetly said, "Be New France true to me
And she shall ever be the home of rugged liberty!"
The vision passed, and the reaper bent to the cutting of the grain;
The covenant is kept; he did not pray in vain.

Reliquary Case, silver, Robert Hendery (1837-1897), Montreal, Quebec, mid to late 19th century. The John and Eustella Langdon Collection of Canadian Silver.

Jean-Pierre Lavallée, Sorcerer (1711)

Île d'Orléans, a large island in the St. Lawrence River, has long had a reputation that gives it the local name of Island of Sorcerers. In 1720 the Jesuit missionary Pierre-François-Xavier de Charlevoix noted:

> *I found this Country fine, the Soil good, and the Inhabitants pretty well at their Ease. They have the Character of being given to Witchcraft. . . . For Instance, If the Ships of France do not arrive as soon as usual, they [the sorcerers] are consulted to hear News of them, and it is said they have sometimes answered pretty true. . . . People believe that they quote from a certain Knowledge. People fancied they had consulted the Devil.*

In the numerous legends involving witchcraft, the practitioners are usually portrayed as malevolent, but here the sorcerer is credited with saving the French colony. R. S. Lambert, in his book Exploring the Supernatural, *found it strange that no historical report mentions this story, but he says that Edward Farrer was a respected journalist who may have obtained it from an oral source.*

Reported by Edward Farrer, 1882

The inhabitants of the Isle of Orleans, just below Quebec, have been charged with sorcery from time immemorial, and as they

Ship in a Stormy Sea, oil on canvas, anonymous, Canada, late 19th century. Sigmund Samuel Trust.

have never sought to purge themselves of the accusation it is doubtless well founded. Satan of course presides at the *sabbats,* or orgies, assuming innumerable shapes and guises. He summons the motley company of sorcerers, damned souls, *loups-garous*, infidels, serpents, and *feux-follets* by ringing a church-bell, stolen while it was yet unconsecrated; and when he has marched round the island at the head of this procession, he presides at the *messe noire* celebrated in his honour, and directs the incantations over the boiling cauldron.

The most famous sorcerer was Jean-Pierre Lavallée, the child of Indian and French parents, who was considered to be skilled at weather lore and capable of casting spells. He is believed to have saved the island from the British in 1711.

No English witch can compare with Jean-Pierre Lavallée, sorcerer of St. François, Isle of Orleans. On the 30th of July, 1711, Sir Hovenden Walker, in command of a formidable armada consisting of men-of-war and transports carrying troops, sailed from Nantasket Roads for Quebec, for the purpose of capturing that post and avenging the repulse of Sir William Phipps in 1690. Paradis, master on a Rochelle gunboat which had been captured by the British frigate *Chester,* was put on board the flagship *Edgar* as pilot, for he knew the St. Lawrence well.

A dense fog settled down upon the fleet after it left Gaspé Bay; and at ten p.m. on August 22nd, "We found ourselves," writes Admiral Walker in his Journal (printed by D. Browne at the Black Swan, W. Mears at the Lamb without Temple Bar, and G. Strahan at the Golden Ball against the Exchange in Cornhill, 1720), "upon the North Shore, amongst rocks and islands, at least fifteen leagues farther than the log gave, when the whole fleet had like to have been lost. But by God's good providence all the men-of-war, though with extreme hazard and difficulty, escaped. Eight transports were cast away, and almost nine hundred men lost."

The beach of Egg Island and the Labrador shore hard by were strewn with bodies. Two contingents of guards, who had fought under Marlborough in the Low Countries, were identified among the dead by their scarlet trappings. Mother Juchereau of the Hôtel Dieu records in her diary that a salvage expedition fitted out at Quebec found two thousand corpses on Egg Island. Be that as it may, it was a wonderful deliverance for the colony.

Some said the French pilot had willfully wrecked the fleet. The clergy held that it was the work of the Blessed Virgin, and the name of the church of Notre Dame de la Victoire in the Lower Town, where Phipps's repulse was annually celebrated, was changed to Notre Dame des Victoires, to commemorate both occasions. But while the habitants doubted not the power of the beneficence of the Blessed Virgin, they ascribed the causation of the wreck to the incantations of Jean-Pierre Lavallée of St. François.

When it became known at Quebec that Queen Anne was fitting out the expedition, he [Lavallée] bade the people be of good heart. He built a hut on the extreme easterly point of the island near St. François, and began his midnight séances about the middle of August; and it is an article of habitant belief that the fog which enveloped the fleet to its destruction was the steam from his infernal pot. There could have been no mistake about this, for when the news of the disaster reached Quebec the sorcerer said that Sir Hovenden had not drained his cup of bitterness; and sure enough, while the admiral was on his way to London to report the disaster, the *Edgar,* seventy guns, blew up at Portsmouth, and all on board, 470 souls, perished.

Thompson Has a Dirk (1749)

Calum MacLeod, who collected and translated many Nova Scotia Gaelic stories and songs, presents this short tale as he heard it in Grand Narrows, Cape Breton. Various tales of non-natives ruling native tribes are known internationally, but this seems to be the only one reported in Canada.

Told by Hugh F. MacKenzie and Mary Elizabeth MacNeil,
undated

> Thompson has a dirk,
> And there are buckles in his boots;
> Thompson has a dirk,
> And well could he use a knife.

Well, indeed, without a doubt, I heard that tune before, and some people from the Old Country used to say that Thompson was related to Lovat, the chief of the Frasers. Well, here is a story I heard about Thompson.

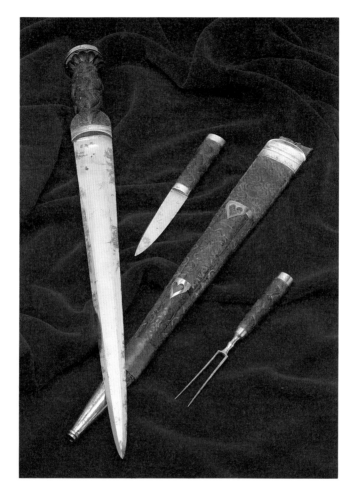

Dirk, steel blade, wooden hilt with silver mounts, leather sheath with metal mounts, anonymous, Scotland, late 18th century. Museum purchase.

In the year 1749, a band of Highland Scottish soldiers was stationed at Louisbourg in Cape Breton County, and on a certain Sabbath Day they went out for a stroll. When they reached the outskirts of the town, didn't the Indians get hold of them! They were taken away to the Indian chief in Eskasoni. When the chief understood where they had come from, he released them, and he told them not to tell anybody in Scotland that he was "Thompson of the Dirk." According to tradition, Thompson fled with his life from Scotland when he had murdered a piper who was playing the tune "Thompson Has a Dirk" at a certain dance where Thompson himself was present. Thompson reached Nova Scotia, and in time he attained the rank of the chief of the Indians. They say that even today, "Thomas" is a common name amongst the Indians in Cape Breton.

La Corriveau (1733~1763)

Marie-Josephte Corriveau, born in St-Vallier, New France, in 1733, was hanged at Quebec on 18 April 1763, for killing her second husband with an axe. Her body was gibbeted—hanged in chains—at Pointe de Lévy. Shortly after her death, legends about her began to circulate, and for centuries tales of her ghost terrified settlers around Quebec.

Luc Lacourcière researched the facts and fiction surrounding La Corriveau, analysing the court records of a controversial court martial in April 1763 that convicted Joseph Corriveau of murdering his son-in-law, Louis Dodier, and named his daughter as an accomplice. When he was sentenced to hang, Corriveau confessed that he had helped his daughter kill her husband. A second trial was held, Marie-Josephte confessed, and she was sentenced to be hanged and gibbeted.

La Corriveau's grim story has been told and retold in many forms. Historically, she had two husbands—the first died in an accident and the second she murdered. But as the tale of her infamy spread it also grew: her crimes multiplied to the murder of six husbands and gruesome details were added.

It is generally believed that La Corriveau was hanged in an iron cage, a practice known in England at that time, but not in France. The iron cage was supposedly discovered a century later and exhibited by P. T. Barnum in his New York museum.

In addition to the many oral versions, this story has been incorporated into various literary works such as Aubert de Gaspé's Les Anciens Canadiens *(1863) and William Kirby's* The Golden Dog

(1877). More recently, Andrée Lebel published a historical novel, La Corriveau *(1981). Marie-Josephte is also memorialized by a bronze statue in the Musée du Québec.*

Lacourcière, who has written at length on both the historical and the legendary La Corriveau, considers that the account of Mme Fradette of St-Raphaël-de-Bellechasse best illustrates the growth of the legend. Fradette shows remarkable ingenuity in reporting the different devices used to kill the various husbands, and a flair for drama in the scene with the seventh husband.

Tales of men who kill a series of women are fairly common in folklore: Bluebeard and the ballad of "Lady Isabel and the Elf-Knight" come to mind. It is interesting that La Corriveau in the legend, like the Elf-Knight, murdered six but was outwitted by the seventh. However, tales of women who kill several men are rare. This is a translation of Fradette's account.

Told by Mme Wilfrid Fradette, 1953

La Corriveau was a wicked woman. She would marry as many men as she could find. She married seven of them. The first had been currying his horse, so she took a large jug to pick up the manure. She gave him a blow on the head. He fell to the ground under the horse. The horse was afraid. The horse kicked him. He was dead. Only a knock on the head with the jug, but it was enough. Then she ran quickly to find people. And, after that, people came. Then they picked up her husband under the horse. It was thought that the horse had killed him.

Not long after, there was another gentleman. The wicked one remarried. That one—she got bored with him—she wanted another one. She poured lead in his ears. Before going to bed she gave him a good drink, a good glass of sleeping potion to put him to sleep. As soon as he was asleep she took the lead which she had boiling there and poured it into his ears. That killed him; it didn't take long, and he was dead. All went like the first time, and she had him buried.

Then she needed a third one. The third one, she stuck a big needle in his heart. To begin, she always gave a glass of sleeping potion. When she wanted to get rid of him that night, she gave him a glass of sleeping potion so he lies down to sleep. She had plenty of time to stab him so he'd die. That didn't take long either. He died not long after. It went like the first ones.

The fourth was given some very strong Paris green, very strong poison, and after he had taken his dose, he didn't wake up. He went to sleep, and stayed asleep.

Then another follows, the fifth. He receives a pin, a big hatpin, in his brain, in his head. She stabbed him with a big hatpin. He died too.

And the sixth, she strangled him. She wrapped a rope around his neck and over the wall to strangle him. So, when she returned from behind the house, when she entered the house, he was dead, strangled. That was her sixth.

The seventh one said [to himself]: "I will marry her, but I will announce what happened to her husbands. It's definite; it is certain that she killed them." So he married her.

After some time she began to get bored with him, too. She prepared for him a hot drink of a sleeping potion before going to bed. When she gave it to him he said, "Ah, good, I am very pleased. This evening," he said, "I am very tired. This will help me to sleep. You are very smart," he said.

So he took his glass and then he waited until her back was turned a little and he poured it out, he threw it on the bed, or — anyway he threw it out. Then he took the glass and pretended to drain it, and he gave it back to her. She was happy. She thought, "It won't be long. He will go to sleep."

So, she wanted to strangle that one too, just as she had done with the other. She took her rope and she had a sliding knot around his neck. He was asleep, snoring, pretending to be asleep. He snored and she approached him quietly. She placed the rope around his neck, and she passed the rope through the door, and she sets it all up, and she goes out, behind the house. And she started to pull on the rope. So, when he saw her go out, he removed the rope from his neck, and he put it around a pillow. So she didn't know about it. When she started to pull on the rope a little he went "Euh! Euh! Euh!" He pulled on the pillow, he pulled on the pillow while crying out. After a little while, he stopped. He pretended to be strangled.

When she pulled, pulled hard on the pillow, and there was no further sound, she came back to see if he was dead. And he was hidden behind the door. Afterwards:

"Why," he said, "did you want to kill me?"

"What—but—" she said. "You're not dead?" she said. "How is this possible?"

"Well," he said, "I have been slyer than you. You see, I must reveal what you have done."

So, well, I don't think they were too affectionate that evening. He denounced her. He was the seventh. So they dug up the ones who were buried. Then they found how they had been poisoned, how they had died. And then they started to talk. It was obvious that they had to put her to death. In those days they did not hang people very much. They killed them in other ways. They found that after killing six husbands she deserved to be put in a cage. They made a great iron cage and then they hung it up with an iron hook beside a road—a highway that went to Quebec. They hung it there. And she died there.

She stayed there a long time. There came a time when her bones became dried by the air, by the sun, by the rain, good weather and bad weather. And then the flesh fell off from drying out. And then the cage cried. The cage cried, "Ein, ein, ein!" Then there were complaints to the council. And then they made the council remove it. It had been there a long time; I can't say how many years. The council asked that she be buried. Then they buried her, I don't know where. And then after that they made it into a story.

My grandfather passed by there and he was afraid. As he came to Beaumont near where she had been, he came from the city and he was very drunk. Then all of a sudden he heard the wheels of his carriage going *tic, tac, tic, tac, tic, tac.* He said, "What is that? What, is it breaking?" He had his bottle beside him, so he takes his bottle, and he takes a good drink. He gets down and looks to see what's wrong with the wheels. There wasn't anything wrong. He gets back aboard and goes on a little ways.

"Ah!" he says, "It's you, La Corriveau, coming to annoy me, it's you. Ah!" he says, "I'm not afraid of you."

Goes on a little ways. Again, *tic, tac*. He continues on, and it gets louder. So he gets off again and again he takes a big drink of dark rum; he looks all around the cart, nothing. His horse was named Gravelle. So he says, "Gravelle, let's go, Gravelle."

So he gets on board again. But his horse is unable to leave. The wheels were blocked. The horse didn't move. "Ah! Well," he says, "I'll stay here." He unhitches Gravelle and puts her beside the road. He says, "There's a little pool near here. You can drink from it." He says, "Leave me be, I'm going to lie down and get some sleep."

So he lies down. He was pretty tired. Obviously he was so drunk, so drunk. He takes a big swallow of dark rum before lying down. And so he goes to sleep, and he dreams of La Corriveau. So La Corriveau comes and approaches him and says, "Come across with me to l'Île d'Orléans. I have to go dance with my friends. Look!" She showed him l'Île d'Orléans. L'Île d'Orléans was all lit up and people were dancing there. He was dreaming, obviously. She says, "I can't cross the St. Lawrence. The devil escorts me everywhere I want to go. But," she says, "the devil isn't allowed to cross the St. Lawrence. He can't carry me across on his back because the St. Lawrence is blessed. Come and carry me; you're able to."

He spends the rest of the night with La Corriveau. He has fine dreams. The next morning he wakes up. Dawn was approaching. He says, "Where am I? In Beaumont, in Beaumont." So he looks at his horse beside the road. She was eating quietly, so, then, he looked at his cart. There was nothing wrong with it. Everything was fine. But then he became afraid; he was much more afraid than the night before. So then he gets back on his cart, and returns home—he lived in St. Gervais—he doesn't dare to speak of this to his parents. Two, three weeks later he told his family. Before that he didn't dare speak of it; he was ashamed.

So after that, well, I don't know, he never returned to her, and didn't dream about her. He didn't speak about it. It was finished.

The Death of Father de la Brosse (1763)

The well-known tale of Father de la Brosse, appears in various French-Canadian collections. Marius Barbeau retold it in English under the titles "The Bell Tolled Midnight" and "Midnight Mass at Tadoussac." He calls him Father de la Brosse. Edward Farrer simplified the name to Labrosse. A person foretelling his own death is a common motif in legends.

Reported by Edward Farrer, 1882

On April 11, 1763, tradition says darkness prevailed on the Saguenay River, the heavens mourning for the death of a Jesuit, Father Jean Baptiste Labrosse, who died at Tadoussac on that day. The story of the miracles wrought when that good man died, as told by Dr. Taché in his *Forestiers et Voyageurs,* and by l'Abbé Casgrain in *Un Pèlerinage à l'Île-aux-Coudres,* is a characteristic Gulf legend.

Father Labrosse was a native of Poitou. He arrived at Quebec in 1734, and for nearly thirty years preached the gospel to white men and Indians along the St. Lawrence and down in the wilds of Acadia. On the night of his death he was at the house of an officer of the trading-post at Tadoussac, and, although nearly seventy years old, appeared to be as strong and hearty as a man of forty.

He was tall and robust, and his long white hair and saintly face made him look every inch an apostle.

At nine p.m. he rose and in solemn tones told his friends that the hour of his death was at hand. At midnight he should die, and the church bell of Tadoussac would announce the news . . . to all the Gulf. He bade the company farewell, charging them, as he left the house, to go to Île-aux-Coudres and bring Father Compain, the curé, to give his body Christian sepulture.

The party sat in silence, listening for the bells, which on the stroke of midnight began to toll. The village was aroused, and the people hurried to the chapel, and there, before the altar, lay the old Jesuit, dead. They watched by the corpse until daylight when the post officer ordered four men to take a canoe and go to Île-aux-Coudres although a dreadful storm was raging in the Gulf and almost choked the wide expanse. "Fear not," said the officer to the fishermen, "Father Labrosse will protect you."

They launched their canoe and great was their surprise to find that, while the tempest howled and the waves and the ice seethed like a cauldron on each side of them, a peaceful channel was formed by some invisible hand for their craft. They reached Île-aux-Coudres—over sixty miles as the crow flies from Tadoussac—without accident. Father Compain was standing on the cliff and as they neared the shore he cried out, "Father Labrosse is dead and you have come to take me to Tadoussac to bury him."

How did he know this? The night previous he was sitting alone in his house reading his breviary, when suddenly the bell in the church (dedicated to St. Louis) began to toll. He ran down to the church, but the doors were locked, and when he opened them he found no one within, and still the passing bell was tolling. As he approached the altar he heard a voice saying, "Father Labrosse is dead. The bell announces his departure. Tomorrow do thou stand at the lower end of the island and await the arrival of a canoe from Tadoussac. Return with it, and give him burial."

And at all the mission posts where Father Labrosse had preached—Chicoutimi, Île Verte, Trois-Pistoles, Rimouski, and along the Baie-des-Chaleurs—the bells of their own accord rang out the death of the old Jesuit at the same hour. And for many a year, whenever the Indians of the Saguenay visited Tadoussac, they made a pilgrimage to his grave, and whispered to the dead within through a hole in the slab of the vault, believing that he would lay their petitions before God.

The Tlingit Encounter with La Pérouse (1786)

In 1786 a French explorer, Jean-François de Galaup, the Count of La Pérouse, led a scientific expedition to explore the Pacific coast of North America. In July, two of his ships pulled into a place on the coast of Alaska now called Lituya Bay. There the French met some natives and persuaded them to trade skins for iron. La Pérouse noted that there was a brisk trade. Then the expedition set sail from the Alaska coast. Two years later it was lost in the South Pacific. However, La Pérouse had left a written account of his encounter with the Tlingit.

A century later, in 1886, Cowee, a Tlingit chief living in Teslin, a small community on the Teslin River southeast of Whitehorse, told American naval officer and amateur anthropologist G. T. Emmons a story of the first meeting of his ancestors with Europeans, a narrative that had been handed down entirely by word of mouth over a number of generations. Here the recollection has been merged with the Tlingit creation myth.

Carl Sagan, an author and astronomer, gave this version, based on Emmons's 1907 account.

Cowee's Story as Reported by Carl Sagan, 1980

Late one spring a large party of Tlingit ventured north to Yakutat to trade for copper. Iron was even more precious for it was unobtainable. In entering Lituya Bay four canoes were swallowed by the waves. As the survivors made camp and mourned for their lost companions, two strange objects entered the bay. No one knew what they were. They seemed to be great black birds with immense white wings. The Tlingit believed the world had been created by a great bird which often assumed the form of a raven, a bird which had freed the sun, the moon, and the stars from boxes in which they had been imprisoned. Believing that to look upon the raven was to be turned to stone, in their fright, the Tlingit fled into the forest and hid. But after a while, finding that no harm had come to them, a few more enterprising souls crept out and rolled leaves of the skunk cabbage into crude telescopes, believing that this would prevent being turned to stone. Through the skunk cabbage, it seemed that the great birds were folding their wings and that flocks of small black messengers arose from their bodies and crawled upon their feathers.

Now one nearly blind old warrior gathered the people together and announced that his life was far behind him; for the common good he would determine whether the raven would turn his children into stone. Putting on his robe of sea otter fur, he entered his canoe and was paddled seaward to the raven. He climbed upon it and heard strange voices. With his impaired vision he could barely make out the many black forms moving before him. Perhaps they were crows. When he returned safely to his people they crowded about him, surprised to see him alive. They touched him and smelled him to see if it was really he. After much thought the old man convinced himself that it was not the god-raven that he had visited, but rather a giant canoe made by men. The black figures were not crows but people of a different sort. He convinced the Tlingit, who then visited the ships and exchanged their furs for many strange articles, chiefly iron.

Bowl Carved to Resemble Raven Holding the Sun, wood, anonymous, probably British Columbia, before 1926. Gift of Mr. Arthur Warren.

The Old Man Who Came from the Sky (1789)

John Meares, a lieutenant in Britain's Royal Navy, resigned his commission to venture into the fur trade on the Northwest Coast. He made three voyages as a merchant seaman, describing them in Voyages Made in the Years 1788 and 1789, from China to the North-West Coast of America. *Meares Island in Clayoquot Sound was named after him.*

  Meares's account of his travels contains a description of the beliefs and traditions of the Nuu Chal Nulth (Nootka). Most interesting is this tale of a stranger who came from the sky with a message for the Nuu Chal Nulth, and of how they came to value copper. The story was told to Meares by "the son of Hanapa."

Reported by John Meares, 1790

On expressing our wish to be informed of the means by which they had become acquainted with copper, and why it was such a peculiar object of their admiration, this intelligent young man told us all he knew, and, as we believe, all that is known by this nation on the subject. Where words were wanting, or not intelligible, which frequently happened in the course of his narration, he supplied the deficiency by those expressive actions which nature of necessity seems to have communicated to people whose language is confined; and the young Nootkan discovered so much skill in conveying his ideas by signs and symbols as to render his discourse perfectly intelligible whenever he found it necessary to have recourse to them. He related his story in the following manner:

He first placed a certain number of sticks on the ground, at small distances from each other, to which he gave separate names. Thus he called the first his father and the next his grandfather; he then took what remained and threw them all into confusion together; as much as to say that they were the general heap of his ancestors, whom he could not individually reckon. He then, pointing to this bundle, said that when they lived, an old man entered the sound in a copper canoe, with copper paddles, and everything else in his possession of the same metal; that he paddled along the shore, on which all the people were assembled to contemplate so strange a sight; and that, having thrown one of his copper paddles on shore, he himself landed. The extraordinary stranger then told the natives that he came from the sky—to which the boy pointed with his hand; that their country would one day be destroyed, when they would all be killed, and rise again to live in the place from whence he came. Our young interpreter explained this circumstance of his narrative by lying down as if he were dead; and then rising up suddenly, he imitated the action of soaring through the air.

He continued to inform us that the people killed the old man, and took his canoe, and that from this event they derived their fondness for copper. He also gave us to understand that the images in their houses were intended to represent the form and perpetuate the mission of the old man who came from the sky.

Such was the imperfect tradition which we received of what may be called the sacred history of their country, and on which the inhabitants rested the common hope of the human mind in every state and form of our nature—that there will be an existence hereafter, beyond the reach of sublunary sorrow.

Tecumseh's Burial (1813)

Tecumseh (1768?-1813), is a seminal figure in native mythology, his influence extending, in some ways, even into the present. His destiny is closely linked with that of his brother, Tenskswatawa, known also as the Shawnee Prophet. Born in what is now west central Ohio, of Shawnee and Creek parents, Tecumseh and the Prophet witnessed from an early age the westward march of the American frontier, through Indian lands, toward the Mississippi. By 1805 the Prophet had begun to preach the need for Indian resistance to the "contamination" of non-native ways, but it was Tecumseh who would transfigure what was in essence a religious revival into a grand effort to forge Indian unity.

Arguing that tribal cessions of territory violated the communal nature of all Indian lands, he had by 1809 built a native confederacy in much of America's "Old Northwest," the area south of the Great Lakes, between the Ohio and Mississippi rivers and including the territory of the present states of Ohio, Indiana, Illinois, Michigan, Wisconsin, and part of Minnesota. Further erosion of Indian lands, culminating in the second Treaty of Fort Wayne (1809) and related, peripheral cessions, aggravated tensions.

As the power and prestige of Tecumseh and the Prophet grew, so did the prospect of American military response. In the fall of 1811, while Tecumseh journeyed among the tribes of the Southeast, enlisting their support, Secretary of War William Eustis authorized General William Henry Harrison, governor of the Indiana Territory, to lead an army against the Prophet, to order him to disband his force, and to attack if *he refused. In an attempted pre-emptive strike, the Prophet attacked Harrison's encampment on the Tippecanoe River in the Indiana Territory. Although the result was essentially a stalemate, the credibility of Tenskwatawa (who had assured his warriors that his magic would shield them against injury) was destroyed, and his movement dissolved. Tecumseh fled to British protection at Amherstburg, Upper Canada. In the course of his alliance with the British during the War of 1812 he assisted in attracting native support to their cause. He was killed on 5 October 1813 at the Battle of the Thames.*

Tecumseh finds a place in Shawnee, American, and Canadian lore, and legends surrounding him are numerous. When the Creek Indians refused to join his campaign he prophesied: "You do not believe that the Great Spirit has sent me. You shall know. I shall stamp my foot and the earth will tremble." Two months later, on 16 December 1811, Tecumseh is said to have stamped his foot—and the first of three shocks tore through some 50, 000 square miles of territory.

The spirit of his resistance to Euro-American ways and his position with respect to Indian lands finds expression, for example, in the Black Hawk War of 1832, the Sioux uprising under Little Crow in 1862, and the Sioux uprising of 1890, featuring Wovoka's ghost dance. American Civil War general William Tecumseh Sherman was named in honour of Tecumseh's humanitarian insistence on attacking only military targets.

Accounts of Tecumseh's death and burial are numerous and usually contradictory. Colonel Richard Mentor Johnson, later an American vice-president, claimed to have killed the Shawnee war chief by gunshot at close range. While the circumstances of Tecumseh's death are disputed, the fate of his body is even more murky. According to one legend his corpse was ensconced in a hollow log.

Many peoples have a story of a great leader who dies but will return at some future time to lead his people to victory. The French have Charlemagne, the English have King Arthur, and the Shawnee have Tecumseh.

Belt Medal, silver, made by order of George III for presentation to allied native chiefs, engraved with the arms of Great Britain—"GR" above coat-of-arms, "Chief Tecumseth" below, anonymous, England, late 18th century, engraved 1811-1813. Oronhyatekha Collection.

Reported by Robert Dickerson, 1982

After the battle, the Shawnees buried Tecumseh in a secret place on a bank beside a creek, distant from the battlefield. Some years later, they returned, intending to exhume the body and take it to Oklahoma for burial suitable for one of his importance. But the creek had often overflowed, obliterating evidence as to the exact spot of burial. Rather than make an extended search at that time, the Indians left the spot.

In 1941, however, his bones were disinterred, reassembled, and placed in a cairn of stones on the bank of the St. Clair River, on Ontario's Walpole Island Indian Reserve. It remains a Shawnee tradition that Tecumseh will one day return and that at that time all Indian tribes will be united.

The skeleton interred with much ceremony on Walpole Island, however, exhibits no damage to its hip bones. As a young man Tecumseh reportedly broke both hips when he fell from a horse, resulting in one leg being shorter than the other. It appears then that the site of Tecumseh's burial must remain a mystery.

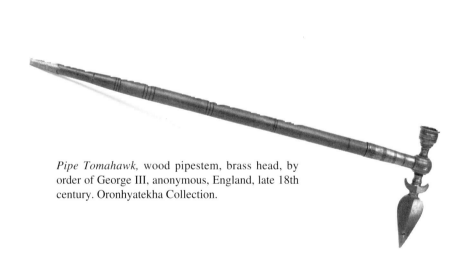

Pipe Tomahawk, wood pipestem, brass head, by order of George III, anonymous, England, late 18th century. Oronhyatekha Collection.

The Fireship Teazer (1813)

Considering how much of Canada's history and geography is bound up with the sea, it is not surprising that we have numerous sea legends. Tales of spectral ships are very common on Canada's east coast. The Fireship Teazer, the most frequently reported, appears here in two versions.

Sceptics commonly explain sightings of the Teazer as oddly shaped clouds or fog. Helen Creighton tells of one day when she thought she saw a boat—a black hull, the white superstructure, and even smoke from the funnels. Then she realized that it was merely a fog, hanging between her and the opposite bank, which gave the impression of a moving ship.

Creighton also mentions a young man who thought he saw the Teazer, looking just like a sailing ship on fire. He and his friends watched it for about two minutes until it sank before their eyes. Their scepticism disappeared. They went inside, and when they came out again the moon was just coming up where they had seen the ship. They realized then that there must have been a bank of fog in front of the moon as it first came over the horizon, creating the illusion of a ship on fire. Probably many sightings of the fireship are explained by similar atmospheric conditions, but some of the accounts are very convincing.

This account is condensed from Archibald MacMechan's Tales of the Sea.

Early in the War of 1812, New York commissioned a small fleet as privateers to prey on British ships in Halifax Harbour. Within a few months the *Teazer,* a small vessel of eighty-eight tons with a crew of fifty, captured a dozen British ships, winning prize money for the crew. In December 1812 the *Teazer* was captured by Britain's North Atlantic fleet and burned. The officers and crew were taken prisoner and paroled on their promise not to take up arms against Great Britain again.

However, the crew's stories of their triumphs led to another ship, dubbed the *Young Teazer,* being licensed on May 3, 1813. Much larger than the first one, it was a fast vessel of twelve tons and a crew of sixty-five. Lieutenant Johnson, who had been on the first *Teazer,* broke his parole and sailed on the new one.

On June 3 she sailed from Portland, Maine, to Nova Scotia's coastal waters, and shortly captured half a dozen British ships near the entrance to Halifax Harbour. Dr. MacMechan notes; "Legend has it that she dashed into the harbour itself and escaped capture by hoisting British colours. This was certainly putting your head in the lion's mouth, but the *Young Teazer* was capable of such bravado." Several British ships chased her but the Yankee ship was too speedy for them.

Then, after three weeks, on June 26, 1813, the people of Lunenburg saw two ships entering the harbour. The frigate *Orpheus* had spotted the *Teazer* and chased her in. The *Teazer* hoped to evade pursuit by sailing between Cross Island and East Point into Mahone Bay. The *Orpheus,* a heavier ship, became becalmed and could not follow, but a smaller square-rigger, *La Hague,* worked to windward, trapped her in Mahone Bay, and sent several boats to capture her. Lieutenant Johnson, who feared he would swing from the yardarm for breaking his parole, set fire to the *Teazer*'s magazine, and viewers on shore saw a tremendous flash and heard a great explosion. The ship was destroyed and most of the crew were killed; a few were rescued although injured.

The memory of the light has not yet passed away. School children of Lunenburg report the tale "authorized by their grandam," and point out where the *Young Teazer* went down. The belated fisherman in his dory, overtaken by fog or night, still reports the apparition of a blazing ship in the gloom. She nears and nears, and then blows up and vanishes. Or out by Tancock, a "fireship" appears with men in cocked hats and strange old-fashioned array. The ghost of the privateer, a local "flying Dutchman," still haunts the coast she raided so audaciously more than a century ago.

Reported by Helen Creighton, 1957

We must go back to the twenty-sixth of June, 1813, when a privateer, the *Young Teazer,* was trapped by British warships in Mahone Bay on our southwestern shore. She would have been captured if a young officer had not set her afire rather than swing at the yardarm. I have talked to people whose parents witnessed the event when they saw a huge explosion as she went up in a blaze of fire. Windows were broken at Blandford, so strong was the blast.

From that time, and never before, her apparition has been reported. The old people would tell about having her sail to within a couple of yards of their boat and filling them with fear because they were sure they would be run down. In one case a fisherman told how she stood directly in his way and he could hear the ropes creak in the blocks. From Boutiliers Point it was reported that the ropes were all on fire. It was seen then coming to East Chester from Quaker Island at two o'clock in the morning. Again some Margaret's Bay men were in a boat near Clam Island when they had to get out of the *Teazer*'s way, and they said they could see the crew in the rigging. I have never heard of any calamity following the appearance of this burning ship, but it often seems to have had a frightening effect.

One day I went to call on Mr. Joseph Hyson of Mahone Bay, a kindly old retired sailor of eighty-eight who had sung me several sea chanties. Our conversation turned to the *Teazer* and he said, "My mother was a Mader from Mader's Cove and she saw it different times, and I've seen it too. One Christmas Eve we were coming from Halifax in a southeast wind. It was dark and a storm was coming up. There was a man up forward looking out, and the skipper had to go forward, too. I had the wheel and one of the men said, "What's that?" and there was a big red light coming up. It looked like an explosion. Could it have been the moon? No, it couldn't possibly have been the moon, not on a night like that and seeing it as we did. The moon!" (Great disgust in that last word.)

As one man said, "I have seen the *Teazer* light as often as I have fingers and toes," and I could say that I have heard that many stories about it. Its last appearance to my knowledge was in 1935.

A Woman Warrior (1828)

Legends of women warriors are found in many nations, and ballads about women who disguise themselves as men are numerous. Some of the stories are true, some are fictional, and some are a mixture of fact and fiction. Here the woman's prophecy at least is legendary, although the story itself appears to have a factual basis.

Reported by Sir John Franklin, 1828

I mentioned in my former narrative that the northern Indians had cherished a belief for some years that a great change was about to take place in the natural order of things, and that, among other advantages arising from it, their own condition of life was to be materially bettered. This story, I was now informed by Mr. Stewart [chief factor at Fort Chipewyan], originated with a woman, whose history appears to me deserving of a short notice.

While living at the N. W. Company's post on the Columbia River, as the wife of one of the Canadian servants, she formed a sudden resolution of becoming a warrior, and, throwing aside her female dress, she clothed herself in a suitable manner. Having procured a gun, a bow and arrows, and a horse, she sallied forth to join a party of her countrymen then going to war. In her first essay she displayed so much courage as to attract general regard, which was so much heightened by her subsequent feats of bravery that many young men put themselves under her command.

Their example was soon generally followed, and at length she became the principal leader of the tribe, under the designation of the "Manlike Woman." Being young, and of a delicate frame, her followers attributed her exploits to the possession of supernatural power, and therefore received whatever she said with implicit faith. To maintain her influence during peace, the lady thought proper to invent the above-mentioned prediction, which was quickly spread through the whole northern district.

At a later period in her life, our heroine undertook to convey a packet of importance from the company's post on the Columbia to that in New Caledonia, through a tract of country which had not, at that time, been passed by the traders, and which was known to be infested by several hostile tribes. She chose for her companion another woman, whom she passed off as her wife. They were attacked by a party of Indians, and though the Manlike Woman received a wound in the breast, she accomplished her object, and returned to the Columbia with answers to the letters.

When last seen by the traders, she had collected volunteers for another war excursion, in which she received a mortal wound. The faith of the Indians was shaken by her death, and soon afterwards the whole of the story she had invented fell into discredit.

The Baldoon Mystery (1829~1831)

The romantic ghosts that haunt English castles are less numerous in Canada, but we have had our share of more down-to-earth ghosts, and many tales of poltergeists—the "noisy spirits" that cause unexplained physical disturbances such as fires, lights, broken objects, or showers of stones. Of Canada's several striking cases, the three-year haunting of a Highland Scots family at Baldoon, Ontario, is the most remarkable. It formed the basis for James Reaney's play Baldoon *(1976).*

  According to eye-witnesses, many strange events happened on John T. McDonald's farm between 1829 and 1831. Neil T. McDonald, John's younger son, collected statements from twenty-six people in the community who knew of these events. He published them in a sixty-two-page booklet titled The Belledoon Mysteries: An O'er True Story, *which was reprinted several times. Neighbours described how bullets came through the windows, household items moved erratically, fires started up repeatedly, the house and the barn were burned, and animals died. Two of the twenty-six statements are printed here. James Johnson mentions one of the more unusual happenings: a pot chased a dog to Michigan. The second account is longer and typical of the group. Accounts of the solution to the Baldoon mystery are included in this and in the next story, "The Witch Doctor of Long Point." The legends are intertwined.*

James Johnson's Statement, 1871

During the years 1829-30-31, I lived within three miles of John T. McDonald's and I used to go and see the balls coming through the window. Being young, it was great sport for me. I wore a Scotch cap at the time and I would gather the balls in it and take them home, and tell mother about the witch balls, as they were called. She would make me throw them away, for she said the witches would come and take me with them. I said I would like no better fun. We used to see a stray goose with a black head and part of one wing black, swimming up and down the river, always quacking as if lost, but after McDonald shot it the mystery was solved.

I have seen the furniture fly in all directions, and the mush pot chased the dog from Canada to the state of Michigan. The pot had been absent for three days, and in four weeks we heard that the dog was found four miles west in Michigan and it never came back to Canada. Mr. McDonald used to trade at my father's store and was always upright in all his dealings.

Allen M. McDonald's Statement, 1871

This is what I heard my father, John McDonald, say he was an eye witness to. He was at McDonald's where these strange things happened and he saw a stone come in through the window and strike a man by the name of Neil Campbell in the breast. Mr. Campbell, being an unbeliever in such mysteries, said in a bragging manner, "Send us another ball, old fellow, and I will catch it." No sooner said than another stone came through the window and struck him in the breast with such force that it stunned him. He was glad to say that was enough, and stood, apparently breathless, and pale as a corpse, and he was satisfied that there was no fun in catching balls in this manner, and like many others, went home convinced that it was no humbug.

Next he [Allen McDonald's father] saw a stone about the size of a hen's egg, and muddy out of the river, come in through the window, and roll on the floor. He picked it up and in a moment, another stone came, as above. Next he was there when one of the buildings was burning and saw on another building near the one that was burning a large black dog sitting there and watching the fire, when all at once he disappeared, and no one could tell how he went. Next a large stone came down the fire-place with such force that it bounded up to the ceiling and dropped on the unbeliever's head. He said it hurt him enough to convince him that there was more truth than poetry in what he had heard, and like many others who went, who did not believe in witchcraft, went home convinced that the handcuffs were off the old fellow, and this was the devil's work.

He next saw the McDonald house set on fire fifty times in one day and helped to put it out every time. Not a spark of fire was to be seen about the house only where the fire broke out and then about fifty men were ready to put it out instantly. Next he saw an iron tea kettle rise off the fire-place and fly across the room full of boiling water and never spill a drop, and the lid of the kettle blew off and struck the window casing with such force that it left a mark of the lid a fourth of an inch deep which could be seen for thirty-five years after it happened. I have seen it myself hundreds of times. Again I saw an auger, which was hanging on a nail, blow across the room and strike the bedpost with such force that it coiled around the post and the print of the auger could be seen for years after.

The next is what John T. McDonald told my father about how he found out who it was that was troubling him. A preacher by the name of McDorman told McDonald that he would go with him; he would take him to a man by the name of Troyer, who had a daughter who could solve any mystery a person desired her to.

McDonald and the elder went to see her, and on the way he said he never heard such fearful noises as he did then. They had to go over what is called the "Longwoods Road," which is twenty-five miles long. Right in the heart of the woods there was a noise like people driving cattle, and noises like fighting, and cries of "Murder! Murder! Murder! Help! Help! Help!" and the night being fearfully dark, he said he never had such a fright in all his life. It seemed more like a week than a night, and the hair of his head stood straight up, and he thought several times he would with fear fall off his horse—for people in those days travelled on horseback—and the largest part of the night's journey was on an Indian trail. McDonald said that the elder was singing as happy as could be and he told McDonald to pay no attention to the noise. He said it was the parties who were troubling him, for they knew where and for what he was going and they wanted to frighten him back, so that they would not be exposed. He encouraged McDonald the best he could, for the elder had the courage of a lion and feared neither the devil or any of his imps, and I believe if there were such courageous ministers on the walls of Zion, there would not be as many wicked people in the world.

When they arrived at Dr. Troyer's, they found his daughter at home and told her what they had come for, and she told them she could give them the desired information after looking through a stone, which her uncle had found in a field while ploughing, as she did not like to look into it as it always frightened her, so that she always had a spell of sickness. McDonald begged of her to look into it and tell him who the parties were, and the cause of his trouble, and with this he would be satisfied.

The doctor finally persuaded her to look into the stone, and on doing so the first question she asked was, "Did you buy a piece of land previous to this trouble?" Mr. McDonald answered yes. She then described the members of a certain family and asked if this family did not live by this land that he had bought. He answered yes. "Did this family want to buy it of you?" "Yes." "And you would not sell it to them?" "No, for I didn't buy it to sell, I bought it to keep for the family."

She then told Mr. McDonald everything that had happened and told him that one of his buildings had burned two hours previous, and they being eighty miles from home set down the time and found on going home that she had told to a minute. She then asked him if there was not a stray goose, with a black head and part of one wing black, with his geese. He studied for a moment and said that he remembered seeing a goose of that description, but he thought it was one of his own. She said, "No, that is the old woman of the family mentioned and she was the old witch. She turned herself into a goose and she was the one that brought up the balls from the river bottom that were marked and thrown into the river."

She then told him that if that goose was there when he got home to put some silver in his gun and shoot it, and if he hit it, it would disappear and he would find the old woman wounded by the silver he had shot her with the day before. When he had done so he found her wounded in the arm. He asked her a few questions in reference to the trouble, but she would give him no answer, for she knew that they were exposed.

McDonald then went home and was troubled no more, but the old woman never had a moment of peace until she died. If she sat down she would jump up and say that she was sitting on a hot grid-iron. She suffered for her bad deeds in various ways. McDonald had nothing left but his land, as his stock had all died and his buildings all burned.

In reference to his character I can truthfully say that I knew John T. McDonald for more than thirty-five years, and I never heard anything amiss with him or his family. He was in good standing in the Baptist church for many years to my knowledge.

The Witch Doctor of Long Point
(1753~1842)

John Troyer (1753-1842) was a remarkable character whose exploits have been recorded in various books and articles. The stories of his witchcraft, which seem to be well documented, display many of the motifs found in other legends. They include a magic stone that enables the owner to see objects at a distance; being tortured and ridden by a witch; using a Bible to ward off the devil; and the devil as a black dog.

Interest in his supernatural powers tended to obscure Dr. Troyer's other very real accomplishments. As Harry Barrett shows, he was a dowser, a pioneer naturalist and orchardist, a herbal doctor, and an early boat builder.

Reported by Harry B. Barrett, 1977

Shortly after 1790 [John Troyer's] cabin stood nestled into the lake bank east of Point Rowan, where a spring-fed brook at that time gurgled through a picturesque ravine. Over the years as this stream had cut deep into the lake bank, it had deposited sand and clay in a broad delta. On the marsh-fringed fertile silt, Troyer, a competent farmer and herbalist, established an orchard and farmed the fifteen acres of flats that, even today, are not visible from the road a few hundred yards north. . . . Troyer was a competent botanist and very knowledgeable about the medicinal properties of the flora of his forest home. He was also unbelievably superstitious. Coupled with this, he seemed to possess extra-sensory perception or "second sight," as well as the ability to use a divining rod or willow to "witch" successfully for both water and metals.

Martha Ryerse, daughter of the founder of Port Ryerse, has described Troyer as a fine-looking man, highly respected for his willingness and ability to cure the maladies of his neighbours. He came to be known affectionately, far and wide, as Dr. Troyer. Because of his other gifts and superstitions this title often became "the witch doctor." The tales of the supernatural that grew up around him were endless. For the sturdy pioneers, most of whom had little time or opportunity for formal schooling, old country legends and superstitions were soon interwoven with real or imagined experiences relating to the venerable enigmatic witch doctor of Long Point.

Perhaps the best known of these tales relate to the good doctor's persecution by witches. He attributed all his mental and physical aches and pains to the evil spells these ladies of the night cast over him. As he grew older his terror of them grew to the point where he bolted a large bear trap to the floor at the foot of his bed and set it nightly to deter them. In spite of such precautions he believed they periodically removed him from his home, transformed him into a wild or domestic animal, and forced the poor creature to take part in their evil activities. He often related how he had been snatched from a peaceful sleep, turned into a horse, and ridden by the tormentors across Lake Erie to Dunkirk, where they attended a clandestine dance. The poor doctor stood tied to a post with nothing but rye straw for sustenance after his exhausting trip, watching through the window the wild ceremonies that lasted long into the night. After this harrowing experience, it took a long, involved treatment with his most potent herbs to help him regain his health . . .

Dr. Troyer, as well as laying honest claim to being a naturalist and our first medical practitioner (though unlicensed), was also Norfolk's first orchardist. In a country noted today for its production of tree fruits, this is of more than historical interest. . . .

Yet another skill of this interesting man is disclosed by his petition in 1797 to construct a dock and small harbour through the marsh in front of his buildings. The following year he advertised for sale a ship built by himself and William Dealy—"a good sloop of black walnut, 38 tuns burthen, with rigging and tackle compleat and calculated for carrying lumber." If this vessel was not the first to be built in the Long Point district, it was surely among the first.

But despite all these useful ventures, it is as a man in touch with the supernatural that Dr. Troyer is remembered in Long Point. One group of stories relates to his gift of clairvoyance, which he shared with a Fick girl who is said to have lived with his family. Their method was to stare trancelike into a large moonstone, in which they believed they could see the location of articles distraught neighbours believed lost or stolen.

The two were credited with solving the supernatural occurrences which plagued the life of John McDonald of the Baldoon settlement on Lake St. Clair. For some three years the unfortunate settler was harassed by inexplicable disasters. Poles in the loft of his barn would become dislodged, falling perilously close to his daughters or wife. Windows in his house would be shattered, as if by unseen missiles, even in broad daylight. Then his crops began to fail, his cattle sickened and die. Finally his barns burned to the ground. At last he finally heard of the doctor in Long Point with a magic stone who could discover the source of the hex.

On reaching the Troyer's cabin, McDonald related all that had taken place. The Fick girl listened intently and then described a neighbour woman, old and widowed, who coveted his land. At this point, the girl retired to consult the moonstone and, so the story goes, gazed unblinking into it for three hours. On returning to the room she reported that she had seen fire among McDonald's outbuildings, but that she also knew the cure to his afflictions. He was to return home, fashion a silver bullet, and load his musket with it. He would find a strange goose with his domesticated flock and he must shoot it with the silver bullet.

Mcdonald returned home and, albeit somewhat sceptical, fashioned the silver bullet. To his amazement he found among his

Pioneer Homestead, oil on canvas, anonymous, Canada, c. 1870. Sigmund Samuel Trust.

snow-white geese one unfamiliar grey one, which he promptly fired on. The goose, struck in the wing and unable to fly, flapped into the cat-tails of a nearby pond, honking wildly, and disappeared from sight. That afternoon, on the strength of the girl's description, he paid a visit to the garrulous old widow, intending to accuse her of bringing his recent misfortunes down upon his head. On entering her yard it seemed unnecessary, for she sat hunched on a bench outside her cabin door, glaring malevolently at him, her right arm obviously broken and supported in a cloth sling. The spell of persecution was ended. . . .

The first account of a search for buried treasure on Long Point relates to Dr. Troyer and his uncanny ability as a dowser for metal. The commonest version of this story comes from the highly respected Simpson McCall, of Vittoria, who was obviously firmly convinced of the veracity of his statements . . .

The treasure was that which trader David Ramsay was alleged to have buried in the dunes near the carrying place, covered by a large black dog. When Troyer heard that Ramsay had never reclaimed his gold, the good doctor took his dowsing rod to Long Point, systematically searched the whole area, and finally pinpointed the location of the treasure. Then one calm warm evening, he had his son Michael rowed up the inner bay to a nearby landfall.

Just prior to midnight, acting under his father's direction, Michael began to dig a large hole in the moist sand. He soon was waist deep in a hole some three or four feet square. His father stood expectantly above him with an open Bible in one hand and a lighted candle in the other to ward off the evil one. On the stroke of midnight Michael's spade clanged dully against a metal object. He dropped to his knees and scraped the sand away to disclose the top of a steel chest. Working feverishly, he sprung the rusty hasp and began to pry up the lid. Suddenly before his horrified gaze a large black dog began to materialize from the chest. He stared for a moment, unable to move.

The faint light from the candle was suddenly extinguished by a clammy current of air, and Michael's terror launched him towards the boat. Throwing the spade in the bottom, he grabbed wildly for the oars and dug deep into the calm waters of the bay as his equally terrified father scrambled over the stern. Few skiffs have ever crossed the inner bay in a shorter time than did theirs that night.

Despite—or perhaps partly because of—such stories, when we try to form a picture of the first permanent settler in the Long Point country, we see an expert hunter, a farmer-botanist of amateur but extraordinary skill, as well as a clairvoyant who used his peculiar talents for good and not for evil in a life-long effort to bring relief from suffering to his fellow man.

A Duel in Annapolis Royal (1830s)

This family legend collected by Helen Creighton recalls the days when duels were common to settle "affairs of honour." As recently as 1835 two members of parliament fought a duel with pistols in Fredericton.

*   The ghostly re-enactment of past events is a fairly common theme in legends. These ghosts appeared in the early 1830s. For another Canadian example see "The Ghosts of Mackenzie House," (page 82).*

Told by an Annapolis Royal woman, undated

When my grandmother was a young girl, about the year 1830 or 1835, there were soldiers here. One evening when the officers entertained, as they so often did in those days, she met a young man and danced with him all evening. They jokingly made an engagement to go horseback riding the next morning and although they had spoken in jest, my grandmother took the invitation seriously, as indeed was intended. She therefore got ready and waited with more than usual pleasure for the young man to appear. Time went on and he failed to come, and she was very displeased. When he finally arrived he looked ashen and distressed. He was full of apologies and told a story that none of them believed. He said, "I spent the night at the inn and, after I had been asleep for a while, I woke up and heard somebody fumbling at my door. The

Girl's Dress, white muslin with trefoil sprigs of beetle wings outlined with thread metal, anonymous, England, 1825-1835. Gift of Mrs. S. Goetze.

door was bolted on the inside, so I knew nobody could get in. But they did get in, not only one man but two. I noticed particularly how they were dressed. They both wore top boots turned down, long military coats, and tricorn hats with plumes. (Uniforms of this kind might be French or English of the seventeenth or eighteenth centuries. Both were garrisoned at different times at Annapolis Royal.) They appeared to be very gallant gentlemen. Then without a word to me, or any sign that they were aware of my presence, they took off their coats, drew their swords, and had a duel right there in my room. I was in such a state of terror that I couldn't speak, and I could do nothing but watch in a horrid fascination. The duel went on until one man ran the other through with his sword, and then wiped the bloody blade on the counterpane. Then, as though that were not enough, he picked the body up and threw it out the window."

Well, how my grandmother laughed, for she supposed the young man had made the story up as a means of retreat from an embarrassing situation. Nothing would induce her to take it seriously, although his white face and nervous demeanour should have been indication enough. The story has been told in our family ever since, and years later when the Royal Bank was built, the body of a man was found dressed as this officer had been described. The inn where he spent the night was near this spot.

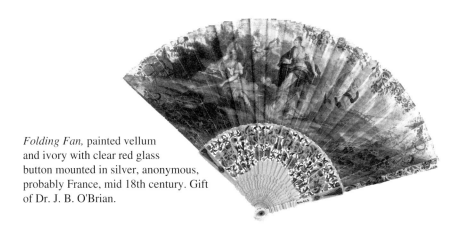

Folding Fan, painted vellum and ivory with clear red glass button mounted in silver, anonymous, probably France, mid 18th century. Gift of Dr. J. B. O'Brian.

The Witch of Plum Hollow (1800~1888)

Tales of elderly women reputed to be witches abound in Canadian villages. Usually the witches are malevolent, like the ones that bedeviled John Troyer and the McDonald family, but Mrs. Barnes was, like Dr. Troyer, a benevolent "witch." She claimed to be "the seventh daughter of the seventh daughter," and hence had second sight and a sixth sense.

Her gift of second sight apparently enabled her to locate lost objects for her neighbours. She became so famous that when George Dagg, who lived near Shawville, Quebec, was being plagued by poltergeists, and decided to consult a fortune-teller, reports R. S. Lambert, "he went off to see a Mrs. Barnes, of Plum Hollow, who had a reputation as the local 'wise woman.' Mrs. Barnes confirmed his superstitions. She told him that his troubles were caused by 'the Black Art,' which was being practised on him by a woman, a girl, and a boy who lived close to his home." She was also said to have helped the police solve a murder case, as this account mentions.

Reported by Ruth McKenzie, 1967

Another woman achieved fame of a very different sort. She was Mrs. Elizabeth Barnes—Mother Barnes, or "the Witch of Plum Hollow." Of course, she was not a witch, and she did not live in Plum Hollow. She lived in a small frame house in the country, not

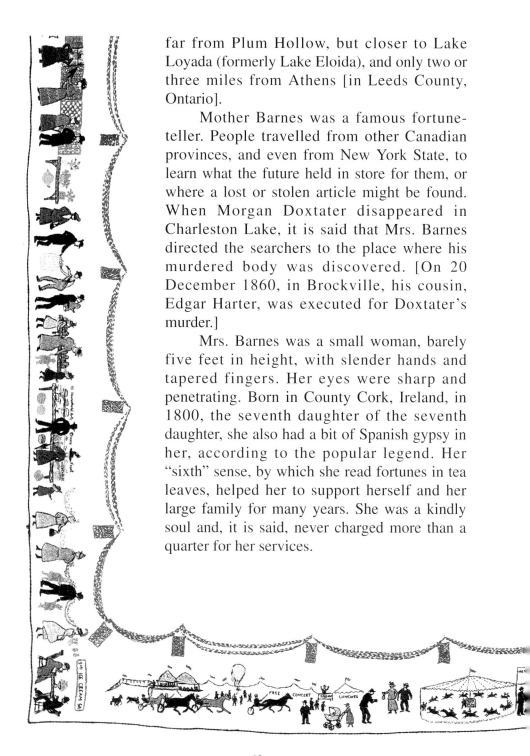

far from Plum Hollow, but closer to Lake Loyada (formerly Lake Eloida), and only two or three miles from Athens [in Leeds County, Ontario].

Mother Barnes was a famous fortune-teller. People travelled from other Canadian provinces, and even from New York State, to learn what the future held in store for them, or where a lost or stolen article might be found. When Morgan Doxtater disappeared in Charleston Lake, it is said that Mrs. Barnes directed the searchers to the place where his murdered body was discovered. [On 20 December 1860, in Brockville, his cousin, Edgar Harter, was executed for Doxtater's murder.]

Mrs. Barnes was a small woman, barely five feet in height, with slender hands and tapered fingers. Her eyes were sharp and penetrating. Born in County Cork, Ireland, in 1800, the seventh daughter of the seventh daughter, she also had a bit of Spanish gypsy in her, according to the popular legend. Her "sixth" sense, by which she read fortunes in tea leaves, helped her to support herself and her large family for many years. She was a kindly soul and, it is said, never charged more than a quarter for her services.

Her personal story was one of romance and tragedy. As a young girl, she eloped with a young Irish sergeant named Harrison, whom her father (a colonel) had forbidden her to marry. The bride and groom took ship to Canada and settled in Cobourg. A few years later Harrison died, and subsequently the young widow married David Barnes, a shoemaker by trade and a native of Connecticut. Six sons and three daughters were born to the couple. They moved to Sheldon's Corners, near Plum Hollow, in 1843. Some time later David Barnes went to Smiths Falls to live, apparently leaving Mrs. Barnes to support herself and family. It was then that she began looking to her fortune-telling as a means of earning money. Her uncanny gift caused her to become known as "the Witch of Plum Hollow," and Thad. Leavitt wrote a novel with that as title. Mrs. Barnes lived to be over ninety. She is buried in an unmarked grave in Sheldon's Corners cemetery.

Tea Cloth, linen tabby embroidered in cotton with vignettes of a county fair, Archie Nixon (designer), dates unknown, New Brunswick, probably 1930s. Gift of Mrs. R. J. Mercur.

Montgomery's Prophecy (1838)

Prophecies that are fulfilled turn up in many legends. Of course, prophecies that are not fulfilled are not remembered, so sceptics are inclined to think that chance rather than magic explains those that are fulfilled. This report adds a legendary touch to the history of the Rebellion of 1837 in Upper Canada.

Reported by Edwin C. Guillet, 1938

When the 1837 rebellion was put down, John Montgomery, a supporter of William Lyon Mackenzie, whose tavern was a rallying place for the rebels, was arrested and charged with high treason. At his trial he was found guilty.

Legend has it that when the jury brought in a verdict of guilty Chief Justice John Beverley Robinson said, "John Montgomery, you have been found guilty of high treason. Have you anything to say before the judgement of the court is passed upon you?"

"I have," Montgomery is said to have replied. "I have not had a fair trial. There are witnesses here who have sworn my life away. The perjured evidence of William Gymer, William Crew, and David Bridgeford will haunt them in after years. These perjurers will never die a natural death; and when you, sir, and the jury shall have died and perished in hell's flames, John Montgomery will yet be living in Yonge Street."

This speech did not deter the judge who sentenced him to be hanged, but on May 25, 1838, his sentence was commuted to transportation for life, and he was moved to Fort Henry. There he and eleven other prisoners organized a dramatic escape and after many close calls managed to reach the United States. There he lived until he was pardoned in the amnesty of 1843. Then he returned to Toronto and lived there until October 31, 1879, dying just before his ninety-sixth birthday.

In his later life he delighted in telling the story of his speech at the trial, and it appeared in his obituary notice in the *Picton Times* of January 29, 1880.

The prophecy was partially fulfilled, for one man shot himself and another cut his throat, and Montgomery outlived judge, jurors, witnesses, and prosecutors.

Chief Justice John Beverley Robinson, lithograph, William Hunt (active 1851-1852), Toronto, Canada West (Ontario), 1852. Gift of Mr. Louis Melzack.

The Mackenzie River Ghost (1860)

Roderick MacFarlane (1835-1920), the Chief Factor of the Hudson's Bay Company, was a member of the Royal Geographic Society, an extensive traveller, and a successful fur-trader. He was thus a reliable person whose account of his strange experience carried more weight than that of another might have done. He described this experience to General Sir William Francis Butler who published it in semi-fictional form in a British periodical, Good Words, *in 1877. MacFarlane wrote out a full account in 1883; it appeared in* The Beaver *in 1939, and was reprinted in 1986.*

John Robert Colombo reports that Lord Halifax told a related version in his collection of ghost stories. It is retold also in Ernest Thompson Seton's Trail and Campfire Stories, *edited by his widow, Julia M. Seton.*

R. S. Lambert termed this "the most convincing of all Canadian apparitions." It is considered "a true ghost story," which suggests that it is more history than legend, but its tale of a corpse that speaks gives it a legendary quality. It might be termed a memorat: a first-hand account of a personal experience, but as it was experienced by more than one man and repeated by others, and acquired variations, it may be termed a legend.

Reported by Roderick MacFarlane, 1883

On the fifteenth day of March 1853, Augustus Richard Peers, a fur trader and post manager in the service of the Hudson's Bay Company, departed his life at Fort McPherson, Peel's River, in the Mackenzie River District, Arctic America. Although he had occasionally complained of ill health, his death after a few days' sickness at the comparatively early age of thirty-three years was entirely unexpected.

He was of Anglo-Irish origin, an able officer, much esteemed by his friends and popular among the Indians. During a residence of, I think, eleven years in that remote district, he had been stationed for two or three Outfit seasons at "Head-quarters," Fort Simpson, and afterwards at Forts Norman and McPherson. In 1849, Mr. Peers was married to the eldest daughter of the late Chief Trader, John Bell of the Hudson's Bay Company. They had two children. In 1855 the widow remarried the late Alexander McKenzie, who succeeded Mr. Peers at Fort McPherson.

While a resident of both Norman and McPherson, the deceased had been heard to express a strong dislike, in the event of his death, that his bones should rest at either spot. Mr. Peers was thought to have made a holograph will some time previous to his demise, but if so, he must have mislaid or destroyed it, as no such document ever turned up.

Having entered the service of the Company in 1852, I was appointed to the Mackenzie River District the following year, and reached Fort Simpson five months after Mr. Peers' death, where I met his widow and infant children. In the autumn of 1859, at the urgent request of Mrs. McKenzie and her husband it was decided that the long-contemplated transfer of the remains of Mr. Peers, from their place of interment at Peel's River to Fort Simpson on the Mackenzie, should be carried out that winter. Mr. Charles P. (now Chief Trader) Gaudet, then in charge of Fort McPherson, agreed to convey the body by dog train to my trade post at Fort Good Hope, a distance of three hundred miles, while I undertook to render it to its final destination, some five hundred miles further south.

Fort McPherson is situated about one degree north of the Arctic Circle. The soil in its neighbourhood is marshy, and frost is ever present at a shallow depth beneath the surface. On being exhumed by Mr. Gaudet, the body was found in much the same condition it had assumed shortly after its burial. It was then removed from the original coffin, and placed in a new and unnecessarily large coffin which, secured by a moose-skin wrapper and lines on a Hudson's Bay dog sled or train, made it an extremely awkward and difficult load for men and dogs to haul and conduct over the rugged masses of tossed-up ice which annually occur at intervals along the mighty Mackenzie River, especially in the higher and more rapid portion of its course toward the northern ocean.

On the first day of March, 1860, Mr. Gaudet arrived at Good Hope and delivered up the body to my care, and I set out for Fort Simpson. The coffin was fixed on one team or train of three dogs conducted by an Iroquois Indian from Caughnawaga, near Montreal, named Michel Thomas (since deceased), while the second train carried our beddings, voyaging utensils, and provisions. I myself led the march on snowshoes, and after seven days of very hard and trying labour, owing to the unusual depth of the snow and much rugged ice, the first two hundred miles of our journey to the nearest point (Fort Norman) from Good Hope, was successfully accomplished. At this place Mr. Nicol Taylor (now deceased) strongly pointed out that unless the coffin was removed, and the body properly secured on the train, it would be almost impossible to travel over the vast masses of tossed-up ice which were sure to be encountered at certain points between here and Fort Simpson. As I had previously gone twice over the ground in winter, and had already had some experiences of *bourdions,* I acted on his advice, and we had subsequently good reason for congratulation on having done so.

After one day's rest at Norman, we started on the last and longest portion of the journey. There was no intervening station at that time, and we met few Indians. The Iroquois Thomas remained with the body train. The baggage train and man from Good Hope were exchanged at Norman for fresh animals and a new driver named Michel Iroquois. Mr. Taylor also assisted me in beating the track for the party, he having volunteered to accompany the remains of his former master and friend, Mr. Peers.

A full description of winter travelling in this country may be learned from the pages of Franklin, Back, Richardson, and Butler [northern explorers who recorded their experiences]. Here it may be briefly stated that we got under way by four o'clock in the morning, dined at some convenient spot about noon, and after an hour's rest, resumed our march until sunset, when we laid up for the night, generally in a pine bluff on the top or close to the immediate bank of the river. Clearing away the snow to the ground for a space of about ten feet square, cutting and carrying pine brush for carpeting the camp, and collecting firewood for cooking and warming purposes usually occupied us for about an hour. Another hour would see supper over and the dogs fed, and by the end of the next sixty or more minutes, most of the party would be sound asleep.

Except on two occasions to be presently mentioned, the train carrying the body of the deceased was invariably hauled up and placed for the night in the immediate rear of our encampment, and except also on the first of the said occasions, our dogs never exhibited any desire to get at same, nor did they seem in the slightest degree affected by its presence in our midst.

About sunset of the fifteenth day of March, 1860, the seventh anniversary of poor Peers' death, we were obliged to encamp at a short distance from *Roche qui trempe à l'eau,* the rock by the riverside of Sir Alexander Mackenzie [the explorer for whom the river was named], as there was no better place within easy reach. The banks here were high, rocky, and steep, and we had to leave both trains on the ice; we experienced much difficulty in scrambling up the bank with our axes, snowshoes, bedding, and provisions for supper and breakfast. The dogs were unharnessed and remained below, while the weather was calm and comparatively fine and mild. The bank rose about thirty feet to the summit where, on a shelving flat some thirty feet beyond, we selected a position for the night. All hands then set about making the camp, cutting and carrying the requisite supply of pine brush and firewood.

Dog Train, White Horse Plains, watercolour over pencil on grey paper, Alexander
Moncrieff (1829-1906), Manitoba, 1857. Acquisition made possible by a contribution
from the Government of Canada under the terms of the Cultural Property Export and
Import Act.

After being thus busily employed for ten or twelve minutes, the dogs began to bark and we at once concluded that Indians were approaching us, as this was a part of the river where a few were frequently met with. We, however, continued our work, the dogs still barking, though not so loudly or fiercely as they usually do under similar circumstances. Neither the dogs nor sleds were visible from the camp, but only from the summit of the river bank. While talking with Mr. Taylor about the expected Indians, we all distinctly heard the word "Marche!" (I may remark that French terms are almost universally applied to hauling dogs and their work in the North-West Territories of Canada.) It seemed to have been uttered by someone at the foot of the bank who wished to drive away the dogs in his path, and we all left off work in order to see who the stranger was, but as no one appeared in sight, Michel Thomas and myself proceeded to the aforesaid summit, where, to our astonishment, no man was visible, while the dogs were seen surrounding the body train at a distance of several feet, and still apparently excited at something. We had to call them repeatedly before they gave up barking, but after a few minutes they desisted and then somehow managed to ascend the bank to our encampment, where they remained perfectly quiet for the night, and thereafter continued as indifferent as before in respect to the deceased's body.

It struck me at the time I heard it that the word *marche* was enunciated in a clearer manner than I had ever before known an Indian to do so, as they seldom get beyond a *mashe* or *masse* pronunciation of the term.

On the eighteenth day of March we were compelled to travel two hours after dark in order to find a suitable encampment, and although we discovered a tolerably good place near the head of a large island on the Mackenzie, yet it was not an easy matter to ascend a perpendicular bank of some twelve feet in height. The baggage train being now rather light, by tying a line to the foremost dog, we managed to drag it and them to the top. The same plan answered with the dogs of the body train; but we considered it beyond our power to get it up, and we were therefore reluctantly obliged to leave it below.

After cutting a trail through thick willows for about thirty or forty yards, we reached the edge of a dense forest of small spruce, where we camped. The customary operations were at once attended to, and when most of the work was over I turned up with some firewood from a distance where I had been collecting a lot for the night.

Mr. Taylor then asked me if I had heard a very loud call or yell twice repeated from the direction of the river.

I said, "No," as my cap ear protectors were closely tied down owing to the cold wind and the thicket very dense.

The two Iroquois corroborated Mr. Taylor's statement, but to settle the matter and find out if any Indian had followed our tracks we all proceeded to the bank, where nothing could be seen or heard, and we at once decided on having the body train hauled up by sheer force, and it proved a tough job to do so.

We remembered our experience of the fifteenth of March, and when we set out early next morning we had reason to congratulate ourselves on taking this trouble, as on reaching the spot from which we had removed the body train, we discovered that a *carcajou* or wolverine had been there during the night. To those who know the power of this destructive animal I need not say that he would have played havoc with the aforesaid remains.

Fort Simpson was at length reached without a recurrence of anything of an unusual nature, in the forenoon of the twenty-first of March, and the body was duly buried in the adjacent graveyard on the twenty-third of the month. Shortly after my arrival, Mr. Taylor and I recounted everything to Chief Trader Bernard R. Ross (since deceased), and the district manager, who had been an intimate friend and countryman of Mr. Peers. Mr. Ross was a good mimic and had an excellent memory. He was asked to utter the word *marche* in the voice of the deceased, and while I at once recognized the tone as similar to that heard by us at our encampment of the fifteenth of March, Mr. Taylor had no doubt whatever on the subject.

During my stay at Fort Simpson, I occupied a shakedown bed in the same room with Mr. Ross, and at a distance from his of some eight or ten feet. On the first or second night after retiring and extinguishing the candle light, while conversing on the subject of the rather remarkable occurrences narrated herein (including the supposed disappearance of his will) relating to the deceased, I became over-poweringly conscious of what struck me then and since to have been the spiritual or supernatural presence of the late Mr. Peers. The feeling, however, came on so very suddenly and scaringly that I instantly covered my face with the blanket and remained speechless. After an interval of perhaps only a few seconds Mr. Ross (whose voice had also ceased) in a somewhat excited tone asked me if I had experienced a very peculiar sensation. I answered that I had and described the feeling which he assured me agreed exactly with what he himself had just undergone. I know from experience what nightmare is; but while it is most unlikely that two individuals who were carrying on a conversation in which they felt a deep interest should be thus attacked simultaneously, it may be stated that neither of us had partaken of any wines, spirits, or anything else which could have brought on a nightmare.

I leave to others, if they can, to give a reasonable account or explanation of the facts I have here stated; but if it be assumed as an axiom that the spirits of some of the dead are occasionally permitted to revisit former scenes and to take more or less interest in their discarded bodies, then from what we have incidentally learned of the late Mr. Peers' sentiments in respect to the final disposition of his remains, what other or more natural course would the spirit of such a man be expected to take with the view of preventing any unnecessary desecration of them than that apparently adopted on the nights of the fifteenth and eighteenth of March, 1860?

From the position of our camp on the fifteenth of March, it may be taken for granted that it was almost impossible to have hauled the body train up such a steep and rugged rocky bank. Dogs are invariably hungry at the end of a long day's travel and as the weather was fine that day, they may have scented the still fresh and perfect remains, and probably desired to get at them, while their barking at and position around the sled would, on any other hypothesis, be at least equally strange and unaccountable. Of course, there was danger from wolves and wolverines, but it is presumed that spirits know more than mortals. On the night of March eighteen, however, although the bank was very difficult of ascent (to get up one had first to raise and push a man till he laid hold of the root of a stout willow by which he hoisted himself to the top, and then threw up a line which aided the rest) it was not insurmountable, and as a most vicious and destructive animal actually visited the spot where we intended leaving the body train for the night, but for the calls and yells referred to, I again ask what other course than that mentioned would any man or spirit possessed of future knowledge be likely to take? And as to the extraordinary feeling experienced by Mr. Ross and myself at the moment when we were talking about the deceased and his supposed will, if it be possible for spirits to communicate with mortals, might this not have arisen (as I actually felt at the time) from a desire on his part to convey some information to us who evinced so deep an interest in the matter but which, from losing our presence of mind, we missed the opportunity of ascertaining?

The foregoing facts made so indelible an impression on my mind that I firmly believe that my present account of them does not in any material point differ from what I communicated to Mr. Ross at the time and repeatedly since to others. I also distinctly remember the occasion on which I gave similar details to General Sir William F. (then Captain) Butler, K. C. B. It was at Green Lake Post, North-West Territories, in the month of February 1873. Captain Butler soon after proceeded to Ashanti, where he experienced a very severe attack of illness, and he, moreover, wrote me that he had taken poetical licence with my narrative, and this will naturally account for the discrepancies between the statements I have given in this paper and his story of same in *Good Words* for 1877.

The Pot of Gold (1865)

The Eastern Townships of Quebec form one of the main English-speaking areas of the province. They were settled by Highland Scots, who came mainly from the Hebridean island of Lewis between 1830 and 1870. They brought with them many of the tales and superstitions current in their homeland, so it is not surprising that they have a great wealth of legends, some old world and some new.

During the American Civil War some young Canadians volunteered to serve in the American army because it was the custom to pay a bounty to volunteers. Some smart young fellows would collect the bounty in one state and then desert and enlist in another state. They were called "bounty jumpers," and a ballad about them was known in Nova Scotia.

Margaret Bennett-Knight, who collected this tale in Milan, Quebec, notes that it is one of the most popular stories told in the Eastern Townships.

Told by Bill Young, 1976

Up in Milan, or near Milan, during the Civil War there was a man who was supposed to have recruited young fellows up there to go and work in the woods in the United States. You heard that one? In return he was getting ten or twenty dollars per man. And, of course, money in those days was either in silver or gold, eh, there was no paper. So these fellows were got together and sent down to the States, supposedly to work in the woods, because the Americans were serving in the army, and were sent south to fight.

So this man made a considerable amount of money, and one night him and his wife were sitting in the house, and they had this money spread out on the table in the kitchen, and they were counting it. And he happened to look up, and—outside the window, there was a man standing in the uniform of a Civil War soldier. And he looked at him so hard that this fellow and his wife took fright, and she swept all the money into her apron and she run and dumped it into a pot—an iron pot that was there. And the next morning, he took this iron pot full of money up into the woods, and buried it.

And, according to the story, it's still there today. And there have been people go to find this, but when they're finally getting close to where this pot is buried, they're seized with such a fright that they couldn't go on. One man, apparently, was picked up by an unseen force and thrown twenty feet through the air, or something, and broke a leg! Now, that's an old one. I think everyone's told that story.

The soldier who gazed through the window and frightened the couple was thought to have been the ghost of a soldier who had been enlisted under this scheme and been killed in battle. Another version of the story added that when the pot of gold was located and the pick or bar hit the pot "there was supposed to have been the awfulest racket—cannons going off and everything, and the regular battles of the Civil War was started all over again."

76

Crippen's Curse (1911)

Dr. Crippen, the doctor who poisoned his wife, is one of the most notorious murderers in the long history of English crime. The story of his murder and his trial has been told and retold many times, and it includes the fact that he tried to escape to Canada, but the story of his curse and its aftermath is less well known.

Reported by Wayland Drew, 1984

The greatest loss of life in the Gulf [of St. Lawrence] in a single wreck occurred on Friday, 29 May 1914. In the early hours of that morning the *Empress of Ireland,* a luxury liner outbound from Quebec, collided with the coal ship *Storstad,* and sank with 1,012 lives.

The disaster occurred on a flat calm during a night that had been perfectly clear; but as the up-bound *Storstad* approached the liner a few kilometres east of Pointe-au-Père, fog swirled off the north shore and engulfed both ships. Both took what their helmsmen thought were precautionary measures, for they had seen each other, but their alterations in course proved fatal, sending the *Storstad*'s prow deep into the *Empress*'s starboard flank. The liner lost steam almost instantly, and her captain could not beach her. Momentum carried the *Storstad* a kilometre into the still night, and when she halted her captain could hear the cries of the drowning "like one long moaning sound." Till dawn his lifeboats gathered survivors. Ships 800 kilometres at sea resounded to the distress calls from Pointe-au-Père.

For the thirty-nine-year-old captain of the *Empress of Ireland,* Henry Kendall, the loss of his ship at that point in the St. Lawrence had ominous significance. Four years earlier, on another ship bound up-river, he had arranged the arrest of escaping wife-murderer Dr. Hawley Crippen at exactly that spot. Crippen had cursed him then. "You will suffer . . . ," he said.

Forty-seven unidentified victims of the disaster lie in a little cemetery between Pointe-au-Père and Rimouski, maintained to this day by the CPR. One hundred and eighty-eight were borne in crude pine coffins up-river to Quebec aboard the revenue cutter *Lady Grey,* a "fairy-white funeral ship." Bells tolled along the river as she passed.

(Left to right) *Mourning Angel,* pine, anonymous, Quebec, 19th century. Gift of Mrs. Jeanne T. Costello; *Trumpeting Angel,* pine, Louis Jobin (1845-1928), Ste. Anne de Beaupré, Quebec, c. 1925. Gift of Dr. H. M. Tovell; *Carved Post Finial,* oak, anonymous, Quebec, 1880. Sigmund Samuel Trust.

The Story of the Newfoundland (1914)

This legend is an illustration of the sailors' superstition that drowned men return to the scene of their deaths. It is based on a tragedy that happened off the coast of Newfoundland in 1914. During the spring seal hunt, the men had left their vessel to cross the ice in search of seals, and when the weather turned nasty they spent two days on an ice-floe. Seventy-seven of them died on the ice. The owners renamed the Newfoundland *in an attempt to mask its identity, but that did not deflect the ghosts.*

Disasters like this were all too common. The captains were determined to come home with a good load of seals and forced the men to go after them despite the weather. Cassie Brown has told the story of this, the most famous of many sealing tragedies, in a carefully researched book, Death on the Ice, *that is as dramatic as a novel.*

This disaster inspired a ballad, but it is simply a story of the tragedy and does not mention the legend Pat Maher of Pouch Cove, Newfoundland speaks of. His tale adds another motif common in folktales: that ghosts visit the earth annually on the anniversary of their deaths.

Told by Pat Maher, undated

It's always laid down in tradition that if a man is lost from a ship crossing the ocean, that when that ship comes to that certain place on the way home, his ghost will board the ship and come back in her. But in 1914 the worst sealing disaster that ever happened in Newfoundland happened. There was a ship to the ice that year; her name was the *Newfoundland,* and she lost seventy-seven men out of two hundred men of a crew. The men left the ship the thirtieth morning of March and they went on the ice to kill seals. A storm came up and it lasted all the thirtieth of March and the thirty-first, and when they were discovered there were seventy-seven dead.

The other ships came in and crews went through the ice and picked up the dead members, and they got seventy-two; five were missing. They were never got; they were supposed to be drowned. So that ship the next year didn't go to the ice at all—she wasn't allowed to go. She had to undergo certain repairs. So in 1916 she was repaired and went out under another name. Her name was the *San Blandford.* And I happened to be one of her crew. So all spring we were separated from other ships, alone by ourselves until the thirtieth day of March. The thirtieth evening of March we steamed up alongside of another ship, the *Terra Nova.* The captain of our ship and the captain of the *Terra Nova* were both brothers. So when we came up it was just dark and a foggy, thick evening and the *Terra Nova* started to blow her whistle. That was a sign that she had someone on the ice—someone that didn't get aboard. So as is the custom, our captain started to blow his whistle too, thinking that they were *Terra Nova*'s men and the *Terra Nova* blew thinking that they were our men.

They heard the men hallo and sing out, away on the ice. So the blowing finally kept up until ten o'clock and one ship stopped and then the other stopped blowing. So the next morning I was one of the men that went aboard the *Terra Nova.* And the first thing they asked me was what time our men got aboard. And I said we hadn't any men on the ice that day. "Oh," they said, "Yes, ye had got men on the ice, because we saw the men. We heard them first hallo and sing out and we watched them until they walked up the side of the ship and went in the boat." Well, we didn't know what to think of it at the time, but some members of the crew declare and solemnly swear that they did see certain men that they knew among what came aboard. So I think that brings the tradition true that men do come home.

The Ghosts of Mackenzie House (1956~1960)

William Lyon Mackenzie (1795-1861) was the first mayor of Toronto and the publisher of the Colonial Advocate, *an early Ontario newspaper. He led the Rebellion of 1837 in Upper Canada, and fled to the United States when the rebellion failed. When he returned to Toronto after the amnesty of 1843, he was elected to the provincial legislature. He lived in a house on Bond Street, and after he died his home, known as Mackenzie House, became a tourist attraction and a museum.*

In a series on "The Ghosts That Live in Toronto," Andrew MacFarlane, a staff reporter on the Toronto Telegram, *noted that two couples had refused to remain in the caretaker's flat at the top of the house. The first couple, the Edmunds, moved in on 12 August 1956, and stayed until April 1960. The second couple moved out after living there for only a few weeks. The following are the sworn statements of Mr. and Mrs. Edmunds and their son Robert.*

This story is unusual in that a ghost is said to have punched Mrs. Edmunds and watered the plants. There are many reports of ghosts that have been heard or seen, but few have been said to be so aggressive.

Told by Mrs. Charles Edmunds, 1960

From the first day my husband and I went to stay at the Mackenzie Homestead, we could hear footsteps on the stairs when there was nobody in the house but us. The first day, when I was alone in the house, I could hear someone clearly, walking up the steps from the second floor to the top. Nearly every day there were footsteps at times when there was no one there to make them.

One night I woke up at midnight. I couldn't sleep, although I am normally a good sleeper. I saw a lady standing over my bed. She wasn't at the side but at the head of the bed, leaning over me. There is no room for anyone to stand where she was. The bed is pushed up against the wall. She was hanging down, like a shadow, but I could see her clearly.

Something seemed to touch me on the shoulder to wake me up. She had long hair hanging down in front of her shoulders, not black or gray or white, but dark brown, I think. She had a long narrow face. Then it was gone.

Two years ago, early in March, I saw the lady again. It was the same—except this time she reached out and hit me. When I woke up, my left eye was purple and bloodshot.

I also saw the man at night, a little bald man in a frock coat. I would just see him for a few seconds, and then he would vanish. I often saw one or the other standing in the room—at least eight or nine times.

A year ago last April, I told my husband: "I have to get out of here." I had to get out of the house. If I didn't get out, I knew I'd be carried out in a box.

I think it was the strain all the time that made me feel this way. I went from 130 pounds to 90½ pounds. I wasn't frightened, but it was getting my nerves down. It was just like knowing there was someone watching you from behind all the time, from just over your shoulder.

Sometimes we'd sit watching the television. My husband might look up all of a sudden at the doorway. I knew what it was. You felt that someone had just come in.

My son and his wife heard the piano playing at night when they were staying with us. When my husband and my son went to look—it stopped.

We could feel the homestead shaking with a rumbling noise some nights. It must have been the press in the basement. We thought at first it might be the subway. But we were too far from the subway. . . . I did not believe in ghosts when I went to stay at the Mackenzie Homestead. But I do now. It's the only explanation I can think of.

I wish to say that I would not say anything against the Mackenzies. They were hard-working people and so are we. They were not hard on us. . . . It's just that the house was a strain on the nerves.

Told by Charles Edmunds, 1960

Certain happenings during the three years and eight months my wife and I served as caretakers of the Mackenzie Homestead have convinced me that there is something peculiar about the place.

On one occasion my wife and I were sleeping in the upstairs bedroom. She woke me up in the middle of the night and said that she had seen a man standing beside her bed.

My wife, to my certain knowledge, knew nothing of Mackenzie or his history. All of the pictures in the homestead show Mackenzie as a man with hair on his head. The man my wife saw and described to me was completely bald with side whiskers. I had read about Mackenzie. And I know that the man she described to me was Mackenzie. He wore a wig to cover his baldness. But she did not know this.

On another occasion, just after we moved in, my two grandchildren, Susan (then aged 4) and Ronnie (then aged 3) went from the upstairs bedroom down to the second floor bathroom at night. A few minutes later there were terrific screams. I went down and they were both huddled in the bathroom, terrified. They said there was a lady in the bathroom. I asked where she was now and they said she just disappeared.

On another night my wife woke up screaming. She said: "There was a small man standing over my bed." She described Mackenzie.

Another night, a woman came up to the bed and looked at my missus. She was a little woman, about my wife's height. My wife said: "Dad—there was a woman here." I told her she was dreaming.

Another night my wife woke up and woke me. She was upset. She said the lady had hit her. There were three red welts on the left side of her face. They were like finger marks. The next day her eye was bloodshot. Then it turned black and blue.

Something hit her. It wasn't me. And I don't think she could have done it herself. And there wasn't anyone else in the house.

On another occasion something peculiar happened with some flowers we had in pots on a window ledge inside the house. This was in winter and we had the geraniums inside. We watered the plants twice a week, on Sundays and Wednesdays. On a Saturday morning we found that they all had been watered, although we hadn't done it. There was water spilled all over the plants and the saucers they were standing in were full. There was mud on the curtains, and holes in the earth as if someone had poked their fingers in the earth. There was water on the dressing table. Neither of us had watered the plants, and neither had anyone else.

We often heard footsteps on the stairs. Thumping footsteps like someone with heavy boots on. This happened frequently when there was no one in the house but us, when we were sitting together upstairs.

The whole house used to shake with a rumbling sound sometimes. My wife is convinced that this was Mackenzie's press. . . .

I am not an imaginative man, and I do not believe in ghosts. But the fact is that the house was strange enough so that we had to leave. We would have stayed if it had not been for these happenings. But my wife could not stand it any longer.

Told by Robert Edmunds, 1960

One night my wife woke me up. She said she heard the piano playing downstairs. I heard it, too. I cannot remember what the music was like, but it was the piano downstairs playing.

Dad and I went downstairs. When we got to the last landing

before the bottom the piano stopped.

It was similar with the printing press in the basement. My wife heard it first and wakened me. I heard it, too. I identified the sound because it was the same as old presses I'd seen in movies and on television. A rumbling, clanking noise—not like modern presses. When Dad and I went downstairs to see about it, it stopped when we reached the same landing. . . .

We heard the piano three or four times, the press just once. I was not walking in my sleep. I heard them. I don't know what the explanation is. I am not prepared to say I saw any ghosts or apparitions. But I can say that I dreamt more in that house than I ever have before or since.

I do not believe in ghosts. But I find it hard to explain what we heard.

Sources and References

The following notes on the individual tales give the source of each tale with comparative references, and the relevant tale types and motifs (see "Index of Types," "Index of Motifs"). References are cited by author and date of publication; full bibliographic listings appear in "References," beginning on page 93.

An Early Account of a Canadian Sea Serpent
Hakluyt 1589. Reprinted with modern spelling in Payne, ed., 1909, and in Colombo, 1988, pp. 7-8.
Motif: B91.5, Sea serpent.

Princess Sheila
Munn 1934, p. 6. Cf. Ryan 1991, pp. 15-22. Wakeham 1987, pp. 1-160.

The Soldier-Peasant's Vision
Farrer 1882, pp. 544-49.
Motifs: V220, Saints; V222.5.1, Church bells ring without human hands at death of holy person; V510, Religious visions.

Jean-Pierre Lavallée, Sorcerer
Farrer 1882, pp. 544-45.
Cf. Colombo 1988, p. 102. Lambert, pp. 51-57.
Motifs: D2140, Magic control of weather; G283, Witches have control over weather; M341, Death prophesied; M370.1, Prophecy of death fulfilled.

Thompson Has a Dirk
MacLeod 1974, pp. 59-60.

La Corriveau
Lacourcière 1973: 228-64. See also Lacourcière 1968:214-42, and 1969:239-71.
Cf. Aubert de Gaspé, p. 259. Aubry 1968, pp. 47-53. Colombo 1988, pp. 85-86.
Motifs: D1654.5, Wagon refuses to move; D1072.0.2.1, Horse enchanted so that he stands still; E272, Road ghosts.

The Death of Father de la Brosse
Farrer 1882, pp. 548-49.
Cf. Barbeau 1935, pp. 125-35; Barbeau 1955, pp. 102-8. Wallace, p. 18.
Type: ML 7070, Legends about church bells. Motifs: D1812.0.1, Foreknowledge of hour

of death; D2141.1, Storm magically stilled; M341.6, Prophecy: person foretells own death; M370.1, Prophecy of death fulfilled; V222.5.1, Church bells ring without human hands at death of holy person; F965.2, Sun darkened at death of holy person; Q147, Supernatural manifestations at death of pious person.

The Tlingit Encounter with La Pérouse
Colombo 1988, pp. 386-88. Sagan, 1980, pp. 303-4. Emmons 1907.

The Old Man Who Came from the Sky
Meares 1790, pp. 269-70. Reprinted in Colombo 1992, pp. 195-97.
Motifs: F30, Inhabitant of upper world visits earth; M300, Prophecies; M301, Prophets.

Tecumseh's Burial
Dickerson 1982. Reprinted in Colombo 1988, p. 270.
Tecumseh's prophecy: Hall 1975.
Cf. Colombo 1988, p. 270.
Motifs: D1960.2, Kyffhauser: king asleep in mountain will awaken one day to succour his people; M301, Prophets; M340, Unfavourable prophecies.

The Fireship *Teazer*
Creighton, 1957, pp. 119-20. MacMechan 1947, pp. 181-94.
Motifs: E421.5, Ghost seen by two or more persons; E510, Phantom sailors; E535.3 Ghost ship.

A Woman Warrior
Franklin 1971, pp. 305-6.
Motifs: M301, Prophets; M325, Glory and prosperity for a people.

The Baldoon Mystery
McDonald, 1910, pp. 32-36.
Cf. Colombo 1988, pp. 124-25.
Motifs: F473, Poltergeist (sometimes identified as witch or ghost) responsible for all kinds of mischief in and around a house; F473.2.4, House burns for no apparent reason; G265.6.4, Witch causes dog to behave unnaturally. See also D931, D1385.4, D1825.2, D1825.9, G211.3.3, G271.4.8, and G275.12 listed for next legend.

The Witch Doctor of Long Point
Barrett 1977, pp. 52-58.
Cf. Colombo 1988, pp. 167-68. Coyne 1891, pp. 11-26. Lambert 1955, pp. 63-68. Owen 1975, pp. 123-26.
Type: ML 3055, The witch that was hurt. Motifs: D931, Magic stone; D1385.4, Silver bullet protects against witches; D1814.1, Advice from magician; D1825.2, Magic power to see distant objects; D1825.9, Witches have power to see distant objects; D2089.3,

Animals magically stricken dead; D2157, Magic control of crops; F473.2.4, House burns for no apparent reason; G211.3.3, Witch in form of goose; G263.1, Witch transforms person into animal; G265.4.1, Witch causes death of animals; G269.3.1, Witch rides man to dance; G271.2.5, Bible used in exorcism of witch; G271.4.8, Breaking spell by shooting bewitched object; G275.12, Witch in form of animal injured or killed as result of the injury to the animal.

A Duel in Annapolis Royal
Creighton 1957, pp. 81-82.
Motif: E572, Ghost walks through solid substance.

The Witch of Plum Hollow
McKenzie, 1967, p. 216.
Cf. Colombo 1988, pp. 215-16.
Motif: D1825.4.3, Magic power to see lost things.

Montgomery's Prophecy
Guillet 1938, pp. 114-20.
Cf. Colombo 1988, pp. 242-43.
Motifs: M341, Death prophesied; M370.1, Prophecy of death fulfilled.

The Mackenzie River Ghost
MacFarlane 1939, pp. 12-15.
Cf. Colombo 1992, pp. 30-36; Lambert 1955, pp. 156-61.
Motif: E545, The dead speak.

The Pot of Gold
Bennett-Knight 1980, p. 111.
Other treasure stories: Creighton 1957, pp. 42-68; Fauset 1931, pp. 88-93.
Type: ML 8010, Hidden Treasure. Motifs: E493.5, Ghost protects treasure; N511, Treasure in ground; N576, Ghosts prevent men from raising treasure.

Crippen's Curse
Drew and Littlejohn 1984, p. 150. Colombo 1988 pp. 68-69.
Motifs: M451, Curse: death; M370.1, Prophecy of death fulfilled.

The Story of the *Newfoundland*
Leach 1966 (recording).
The ballad: "The *Newfoundland* Disaster," Peacock 1965, pp. 967-68.
The book: Brown and Horwood 1974.
Motifs: E271.4, Ghosts of dead sailors go aboard ship passing their burial spot, take stations as crew; E510, Phantom sailors. E585.4, Ghost visits earth yearly.

The Ghosts of Mackenzie House
MacFarlane 1960. Colombo 1988, pp. 252-54.
Motifs: E402.1.2, Footsteps of invisible ghost heard; E421.5, Ghost seen by two or more persons; E422.3.1, Ghost as small man; E425.1.1, Ghost as lady in white; E542.1, Ghostly fingers leave mark on person's body; E554, Ghost plays musical instrument.

Index of Types

The numbers are from Christiansen, R. Th., *The Migratory Legends: A Proposed List of Types*. Helsinki: Suomalainen Tiedeakatemia, 1958.

ML 3055	The witch that was hurt.
ML 7070	Legends about church bells.
ML 8010	Hidden treasure.

Index of Motifs

The numbers are from Stith Thompson, *Motif-Index of Folk Literature*, 6 vols. 2nd ed., Bloomington, Ind.: University of Indiana Press, 1961; and Ernest W. Baughman, *Type and Motif Index of the Folktales of England and North America*, The Hague: Mouton, 1966.

B91.5	Sea serpent.
D931	Magic stone.
D1273.1.1	Three as magic number.
D1385.4	Silver bullet protects against witches.
D1654.5	Wagon refuses to move.
D1812.0.1	Foreknowledge of hour of death.

D1814.1	Advice from magician.
D1825.2	Magic power to see distant objects.
D1825.4.3	Magic power to see lost things.
D1825.9	Witches have power to see distant sights.
D1960.2	Kyffhauser: king asleep in mountain will awaken one day to succour his people.
D.1072.0.2.1	Horse enchanted so that he stands still.
D2089.3	Animals magically stricken dead.
D2140	Magic control of weather.
D2141.1	Storm magically stilled.
D2157	Magic control of crops.
E271.4	Ghosts of dead sailors go aboard ship passing their burial spot, take stations as crew.
E272	Road ghosts.
E402.1.2	Footsteps of invisible ghost heard.
E421.5	Ghost seen by two or more persons.
E422.3.1	Ghost as small man.
E425.1.1	Ghost as lady in white.
E493.5	Ghost protects treasure.
E510	Phantom sailors.
E535.3	Ghost ship.
E542.1	Ghostly fingers leave mark on person's body.
E545	The dead speak.
E554	Ghost plays musical instrument.
E572	Ghost walks through solid substance.
E585.4	Ghost visits earth yearly.
F30	Inhabitant of upper world visits earth.
F473	Poltergeist (sometimes identified as witch or ghost) responsible for all kinds of mischief in and around a house.
F473.2	Poltergeist causes objects to act contrary to their nature.
F473.2.4	House burns for no apparent reason.
F965.2	Sun darkened at death of holy person.
G211.3.3	Witch in form of goose.
G263.1	Witch transforms person into animal.
G265.4.1	Witch causes death of animals.
G265.6.4	Witch causes dog to behave unnaturally.
G269.3.1	Witch rides man to dance.
G271.2.5	Bible used in exorcism of witch.
G271.4.8	Breaking spell by shooting bewitched object.

G275.12	Witch in form of animal injured or killed as result of the injury to the animal.
G283	Witches have control over weather.
K1837	Disguise of woman in man's clothes.
M300	Prophecies.
M301	Prophets.
M325	Glory and prosperity for a people.
M340	Unfavourable prophecies.
M341	Death prophesied.
M341.6	Prophecy: person foretells own death.
M370.1	Prophecy of death fulfilled.
M451	Curse: death.
N511	Treasure in ground.
N511.1.8	Treasure buried in chest.
N576	Ghosts prevent men from raising treasure.
Q147	Supernatural manifestations at death of pious person.
V220	Saints.
V222.5.1	Church bells ring without human hands at death of holy person.
V510	Religious visions.

References

Aubry, Claude. *The Magic Fiddler and Other Legends of French Canada.* Toronto: Peter Martin Associates, 1968.

Barbeau, Marius. *The Kingdom of the Saguenay.* Toronto: Macmillan, 1935.
—. *The Tree of Dreams.* Toronto: Oxford University Press, 1955.
Barrett, Harry B. *Lore and Legends of Long Point.* Toronto: Burns and MacEachern, 1977.
Baughman, Ernest W. *Type and Motif Index of the Folktales of England and North America.* The Hague: Mouton, 1966.
Bennett-Knight, Margaret. "Folkways and Religion of the Quebec Hebridean Homes." In *Cultural Retention and Demographic Change: Studies of the Hebridean Scots in the Eastern Townships of Quebec,* ed. Laurel Doucette. Ottawa: National Museums of Canada, 1980.
Brown, Cassie, with Harold Horwood. *Death on the Ice.* Toronto: Doubleday, 1974.
Butler, William F. *Good Words,* vol. 18. London: Daldy, Isbister and Co., 1877.

Christiansen, R. Th. *The Migratory Legends: A Proposed List of Types.* Helsinki: Suomalainen Tiedeakatemia, 1958. Reprinted. New York: Arno Press, 1977.
Colombo, John Robert. *Dark Visions.* Toronto: Hounslow, 1992.
—. *Mysterious Canada.* Toronto: Doubleday, 1988.
Creighton, Helen. *Bluenose Ghosts.* Toronto: Ryerson, 1957.

Dickerson, Robert B., Jr. *Final Placement: A Guide to the Deaths, Funerals, and Burials of Famous Americans.* Aldonac, Mich.: Reference Pub., 1982.
Dorson, Richard. *American Folklore and the Historian.* Chicago: University of Chicago Press, 1959.
Doucette, Laurel, ed. *Cultural Retention and Demographic Change: Studies of the Hebridean Scots in the Eastern Townships of Quebec.* Canadian Centre for Folk Culture Studies. National Museum of Man, Mercury Series, No. 34. Ottawa: National Museum of Man, 1980.
Drake, Benjamin. *Life of Tecumseh and His Brother the Prophet.* Cincinnati, Ohio: E. Morgan and Co., 1841.
Drew, Wayland, and Bruce Littlejohn. *A Sea Within: The Gulf of St. Lawrence.* Toronto: McClelland and Stewart, 1984.
Dundes, Alan. "On the Psychology of Legend." *American Folk Legend: A Symposium,* ed. Wayland Hand. Berkeley: University of California Press, 1971.

Emmons, G. T. *The Chilkat Blanket.* New York: Memoirs of the American Museum of Natural History, no. 3, 1907.

Farrer, Edward. "The Folklore of Lower Canada." *Atlantic Monthly* 49 (April 1882): 544-49.

Fauset, Arthur Huff. *Folklore from Nova Scotia.* New York: American Folklore Society, 1931.

Franklin, Sir John. *Narrative of a Second Expedition to the Shores of the Polar Sea.* 1828. Reprinted. Edmonton: Hurtig, 1971.

Gaspé, Philippe-Joseph Aubert de. *Les Anciens Canadiens.* Quebec: Desbarats et Derbishire, 1863. Trans. C. G. D. Roberts as *Canadians of Old.* New York: Appleton and Co., 1890. Reprinted. Toronto: McClelland and Stewart, 1974.

Georges, Robert A. "The General Concept of Legend: Some Assumptions to be Reexamined and Reassessed." In *American Folk Legend: A Symposium,* ed. Wayland Hand, pp. 1-20. Berkeley: University of California Press, 1971.

Guillet, Edwin C. *The Lives and Times of the Patriots.* Toronto: Nelson, 1938.

Hakluyt, Richard, *The Principal Navigations, Voyages, Traffics, and Discoveries of the English Nation,* 3 vols. 1598-1600.

Hall, Angus. *Signs of Things to Come.* New York: Doubleday, 1975.

Halpert, Herbert. "Definition and Variation in Folk Legend." In *American Folk Legend: A Symposium,* ed. Wayland Hand. Berkeley: University of California Press, 1971.

Hand, Wayland D., ed. *American Folk Legend: A Symposium.* Berkeley: University of California Press, 1971.

Horsman, Reginald. *Expansion and American Indian Policy, 1783-1812.* East Lansing, Mich.: Michigan State University Press, 1967.

Kirby, William. *The Golden Dog.* New York: Lovell, Adam, Wesson, 1877.

Lacourcière, Luc. "Présence de la Corriveau." *Cahiers des Dix,* 38(1973): 228-64.

—. "Le triple destin de Marie-Josephte Corriveau (1733-1763)," *Cahiers des Dix,* 33(1968): 214-42.

—. "Le destin posthume de la Corriveau," *Cahiers des Dix* 34(1969): 239-71.

Lambert, R. S., *Exploring the Supernatural.* Toronto. McClelland and Stewart, 1955.

Leach, MacEdward. *Songs from the Outports of Newfoundland.* New York: Folkways 4075, 1966.

Leavitt, Thaddeus W. H. *The Witch of Plum Hollow.* Toronto: Wells Publishing Co., 1892.

Lebel, Andrée. *La Corriveau.* Montreal: Libre Expression, 1981.

MacFarlane, Andrew. The *Toronto Telegram,* 28 June 1960.

MacFarlane, Roderick. "Ghost Story." *The Beaver,* Sept. 1939; Dec. 1986-Jan. 1987.

MacLeod, C. I. N. *Stories from Nova Scotia.* Antigonish, N.S.: Formac, 1974.

MacMechan, Archibald M. *Tales of the Sea.* Toronto: McClelland and Stewart, 1947.

McDonald, Neil. *The Belledoon Mysteries: An O'er True Tale.* Marine City, Mich.: Reporter Book Publishing House, 1880. Reprinted as *The Belledoon Mysteries: A Wierd [sic] Tale of the Early Scotch Settlers of Baldoon.* 3rd edition. Wallaceburg, Ont.: W. Colwell, 1910.

McKenzie, Ruth. Leeds and Grenville: *Their First Two Hundred Years.* Toronto: McClelland and Stewart, 1967.

Meares, John. *Voyages Made in the Years 1788 and 1789, from China to the North-West Coast of America.* London: Logographic Press, 1790.

Morgan, Dorothy. *The Witch of Plum Hollow: A One-Act Play on a Canadian Legend.* Cornwall, Ont.: Vesta Publications, 1977.

Munn, W. A. "History of Harbour Grace—Chapter Five—Colonization." *Newfoundland Quarterly* 34.3(1934): 6.

Owen, A. R. G. *Psychic Mysteries of Canada.* Toronto: Fitzhenry & Whiteside, 1975.

Payne, Edward John, ed. *Voyages of Drake and Gilbert: Select Narratives from the Principal Navigations of Hakluyt.* Oxford: Clarendon Press, 1909.

Peacock, Kenneth. *Songs of the Newfoundland Outports.* 3 vols. Ottawa: National Museum of Canada, 1965.

Reaney, James. *Baldoon.* Erin, Ont.: Porcupine's Quill, 1976.

Ryan, D. W. S. *Legends of Newfoundland and Labrador.* St. John's: Jespeson, 1991.

Sagan, Carl. *Cosmos.* New York: Random House, 1980.

Seton, Ernest Thompson. *Ernest Thompson Seton's Trail and Campfire Stories.* New York: Appleton-Century, 1940.

Sugden, John. *Tecumseh's Last Stand.* Norman, Okla.: University of Oklahoma Press, 1985.

Thompson, Stith. *Motif-Index of Folk Literature,* 6 vols. 2nd ed. Bloomington: University of Indiana Press, 1961.

Wakeham, P. J. *The Legend of Princess Sheila.* St. John's: Creative Publishers, 1987.

Wallace, Paul A. *Baptiste Larocque: Legends of French Canada.* Toronto: Musson, 1923.

Index of Legends